ENDORSEMENTS

My friend Pastor Larry Stockstill lives what he teaches. Through integrity and humility, he has established a legacy of honor, influence, and power. *Model Man* is an essential read for every man who wants to do the same.

JOHN BEVERE
Author/minister
Messenger International
Colorado Springs/United Kingdom/Australia

If anybody knows how to take the journey from integrity to legacy, it's Larry Stockstill. I'm so glad he's written *Model Man* as a road map for the rest of us!

GREG SURRATT
Pastor of Seacoast Church
Mt. Pleasant, SC

In a world of personal failure, mediocrity, and shortcuts to success, Larry Stockstill gets to the heart of what makes the man we all want to be. Larry is the man to write such a book. His life of great exploits and integrity is one of a model man.

TOMMY BARNETT
Phoenix First Assembly
Los Angeles Dream Center

This book is so needed right now! More than ever, we need to be challenged as men to live the lives Christ designed for us. We can be a model man in a world that tries to convince us to be mediocre. Pastor Larry is a prophetic voice to all of us, and I am grateful for his influence in my life.

BRADY BOYD
Pastor, New Life Church
Colorado Springs, Colorado
Author of *Addicted to Busy*

Larry Stockstill knows that when men take their rightful place, things fall into place. *Model Man* by Pastor Larry Stockstill is an essential, insightful, and timely message. Our world is aching for the model man, and this book is paramount for its healing.

STEVE VAGGALIS
Destiny Worship Center
Destin, Florida

In a world of confusion, disorder, and disappointment in the example of leaders, it is refreshing to hear a call back to simply becoming a model for people to emulate. My experience in the business, athletic, and spiritual worlds have taught me that these principles can shape a man into someone God can reproduce thousands of times. I encourage you to read this book and become a model man.

JOHN C. MAXWELL
Best-selling author and speaker

Larry Stockstill writes a compelling message on what we as men must model. Here in the Indiana District

Assemblies of God, one of our core values is TEAM. The *M* stand for "model." I believe what we model in private is what God reproduces in our lives, families, and ministries. I love Larry and the great ministry he has poured into our hundreds of ministers in Indiana.

DONALD GIFFORD
Superintendent
Indiana District Assemblies of God

There is no greater crisis in the world than the condition of the average man. When you consider the number of men who are unfaithful in marriage, abandoning their children, hooked on porn, and financially irresponsible, it is staggering. And that is Christian men! There is no greater challenge than giving our men transformational tools like this powerful book, *Model Man*, to turn things around. Thanks to Larry Stockstill, who is a model man, we have hope. This is a book every man needs in his life.

MIKE HAYES
New Covenant Church
Carrollton, TX

It is with deep conviction I affirm Larry Stockstill's new book *Model Man*. There is nothing more critical or effective than to see a man become a *real* man—real by the wisdom of our creator's plan and purpose-filled values, and by the real power of God's Spirit breathing His life into a man who welcomes His grace and "new man" capability. Larry's a dynamically qualified writer and speaker. Read *Model Man*, and if you have a chance, attend one of his Remnant conferences.

PASTOR JACK W. HAYFORD
Chancellor, the King's University
Van Nuys, CA

Pastor Larry Stockstill has hit the ball out of the park with his new book, *Model Man*. Too many Christian men are not finishing well, so it is refreshing and empowering to read a book that challenges men to take seriously their role as a Christ-fearing leader, a role that starts at home and progresses into their sphere of influence. I have personally witnessed Pastor Larry live and model a life of integrity for the last ten years. He has set an example that has encouraged me to lead my network of churches with integrity, compassion, and love. Let this book be a challenge to model the greatness that God intended for you.

PASTOR RICK CIARAMITARO
President of Open Bible Faith Fellowship
Windsor, ON

Pastor Larry Stockstill is a man of great character and integrity who has a heart for raising up the next generation of godly men. He has his hand on the pulse of culture and understands the crying need for men to rise up and be servant leaders in their homes, businesses, and communities. There's no greater man to lead this charge than Pastor Larry. *Model Man* is a must-read and is an overflow of Larry's life, family, and ministry.

Steve Robinson
Church of the King
Mandeville, LA

Pastor Larry Stockstill is a living example of the model man about whom he writes. His life is a wonderful book we all can read. Any man who wishes to be an effective and successful father and husband will benefit from reading this outstanding book.

Bishop Charles E. Blake, Sr.
Pastor, West Angeles Church of God in Christ
Los Angeles, CA

In a world plagued by moral and ethical failure, we need to be men who will stand up for the truth and live admirable, godly lives. In his book *Model Man,* Larry gives great wisdom and counsel to men about leaving a legacy of honor and integrity for those who will follow them. This is a must-read for all men striving to be a man worth modeling.

Dr. Tom Mullins
Founding Pastor, Christ Fellowship
Palm Beach Gardens, FL

Pastor Larry Stockstill has modeled leadership along with the most unmovable integrity that I have ever been around. There is no other pastor on the planet who can teach the subject of being a model man with more authority or passion. For decades, I have personally seen the impact Pastor Larry has had in transforming weak men into warriors for Christ. When men reach their godly potential, it changes families, churches, workplaces, and even the world. This book inspires and motivates men to leave mediocrity and stretch for greatness. Thank you, my mentor, pastor, and friend.

Rick Bezet
New Life Church
Little Rock, AR

Normally the phrase *Image is everything* carries a negative connotation. But in *Model Man*, Pastor Larry Stockstill proves that it really is true. However, it's not the perfection of our own image that'll give us the life we desire; it's relentlessly pursuing the perfect image of Christ. As a good friend of Larry's for years, I have watched him lead a life that truly reflects what he teaches. His book will, without a doubt, challenge you to live a life of integrity and will convince you that a great legacy is possible for you and your family.

Jim Graff
Lead Pastor of Faith Family Church
Founder of the Significant Church Network

Larry Stockstill's message cuts to the core of our nation's crisis—a lack of consistent, godly men standing up to the tidal wave of immorality that's threatening to engulf us. Without a revival of Model Men we are doomed to drown in the sea of depravity.

Dr. Tim Clinton.
Author and President of American Association of Christian Counselors

Larry would not want me to say this, but Larry Stockstill is the model man. I've seen him mentor and come alongside many people over the years I've known him, so it's natural for him to share his knowledge and advice in *Model Man*. In the book, he takes on the role of a coach to show us how we can become model men—in our homes, workplaces and churches. This short, quick read provides practical tips about leadership while inspiring men everywhere to step up and leave a legacy of integrity.

Robert Morris
Founding Senior Pastor, Gateway Church
Southlake, TX
Bestselling author of *The Blessed Life, From Dream to Destiny,* and *The God I Never Knew*

In a world where media uses fathers as jokes and disappointments, men are looking for guidance and encouragement about what a man after God's own heart looks like today. In *Model Man*, Pastor Larry defines what the Bible says about the man that Christ lived and died for you to become. Every area of your life will be tested, marriage, finances, friendships, parenting and spirituality. Your life is a marathon, and to run a marathon, you need a plan. This book will help you build a plan of success.

PASTOR JOE CHAMPION
Senior Pastor, Celebration Church
Austin, TX

Larry Stockstill is a father in the faith who powerfully models a life of character and substance. This book will inspire and equip men with the principles they need to lead their lives the same way. Time to step up and lead the way, men! Read this book today!

STOVALL WEEMS
Senior Pastor, Celebration Church
Jacksonville, FL

OTHER BOOKS AND RESOURCES BY LARRY STOCKSTILL

Model Man DVD Small Group Series

Model Man Study Guide

Model Man: 50 Small Group Lessons

The One Year Devotional

The Remnant

The Surge

He Teaches My Hands To War

The Power Of The Cross

MODEL MAN

From Integrity to Legacy

LARRY STOCKSTILL

DEDICATION

TO MY PRECIOUS father, Pastor Roy Stockstill, my role model and example in life. I felt the strength of your character, consistency, and connection flowing inside me the entire time I wrote this book. I have never seen you deviate from being a godly model to me in my over sixty years of life. Your model is now affecting a new generation and will affect generations to come.

AUTHOR'S NOTE

FIVE YEARS AGO I wrote the book *The Remnant: Restoring the Call to Personal Integrity.*

Since that time, we have given away well over one hundred thousand copies of that book to pastors and staff in many nations and six languages. Our team has worked for five years with pastors worldwide, finishing twelve Remnant conferences in strategic areas of the United States in 2013. We had 3,786 pastors and staff attend those events. (Some of the thoughts in the opening chapters of this book will be based upon that book, and I highly recommend you read it as a sequel to this one.) Now it is time for a movement of model men worldwide who can shape the destiny of our world in the twenty-first century.

ACKNOWLEDGMENTS

Melanie—For putting up with almost four decades of character formation within me. For raising our six children as your highest priority. For living an unshakeable life through some of the most horrific storms anyone could go through. For smiling in this new season of life with a sense of satisfaction. You deserve a great reward! You are a model woman.

My children—For all six of you, who serve the Lord with honor in the house of the Lord. For your spouses who have become our new daughters and son. For our fellowship as a family as a new generation comes on the scene!

The Surge team—The twelve of you have helped me sharpen my missions vision to a fine edge in the last thirteen years. We have planted over twenty thousand churches together, and the best is yet to come.

The Remnant team—We have had many, many monthly conference calls, conferences, and one-day meetings for pastors. Keep living model lives.

Max Davis—Many thanks to Max Davis who came in and re-edited *Model Man* to make it "pop." You were a joy to work with and did an outstanding job.

The business luncheon guys—Without you, the vision for *Model Man* would never have happened. Thanks for showing up by the hundreds week after week, encouraging me with the realization that men truly are hungry to pursue excellence.

The Bethany family—I pastored you for twenty-eight years and would lay down my life for you. Your infectious joy, community, and passion for souls are legendary.

My Bethany "sons"—To all of the model men who were once part of our twenty-eight pastors on staff and have gone on to plant some of the greatest churches in the United States today. My goal is to be a model man for you as long as the Lord gives me life.

CONTENTS

FOREWORD

BEHIND EVERY GREAT man is a great...*man*.

I know that's not how the saying goes—and I'm certainly not slighting my wife, my mom, and the many other great women who have invested in me and played a key role in my life. However, the greatest influences of my life have been other men. I think that's the way God designed it.

I am very blessed to have had a God-fearing and loving dad, Robert Hodges. He taught me so much about life, family, and finances. He served with me in ministry and went to be with the Lord in 2010. I also had an incredible relationship with my father-in-law, Billy Hornsby. He was my closest friend for so many years until he went to be with the Lord in March of 2011. Billy taught me so much about ministry, attitude, and how to treat people. Now that they are both in heaven, I find myself frequently quoting Dad and Billy and desiring to keep their legacies alive.

Another key man in my life is the author of this book. Larry Stockstill has been my pastor for over thirty-five years. In areas of marriage, family, finances, lifestyle, reputation, and more importantly love for God and people, there are few who are his equal. I've not only learned a lot, but I've also been able to observe his example firsthand.

I came on staff at Bethany Church in January 1984 at the age of twenty. I had a passion to do ministry but knew very little about it. I had five semesters of an accounting degree and was enrolled in a local Bible college, but the best education I received in ministry came from what I witnessed in Pastor Larry's leadership. For example, I didn't learn about prayer from any class. I learned by sneaking into the main auditorium of Bethany at 4:30 a.m. on a Sunday morning to watch Pastor Larry pray. It was life changing to see him spend time with God for three hours—walking through the room putting his hands on every pew, kneeling on the stage behind the pulpit, and crying out to God for people to be saved.

The older I get, the more I realize just how blessed I am to have these men's examples as the foundation for my own. But my stories of fathers and spiritual fathers may not be very encouraging to you, especially if you haven't had relationships like these. Unfortunately, for many men their greatest disappointments and wounds come from men who were supposed to be an example, a mentor, a father to them but weren't.

And that's why I'm so thankful for this book. I believe God is going to impart something to you that may have been missing in your life for a long time. You're going to be able to glean from the life and wisdom of a true spiritual father.

The apostle Paul said you may have ten thousand instructors, but you do not have many fathers (1 Cor. 4:15). Well, now you have at least one. Don't just read this book. Let it serve as a living example of a model man—a father who has something to say, something to teach you. I pray that you not only receive deep within you the seeds of truth in this book, but that you also catch the spirit and DNA of a true model man.

Get ready to grow!

CHRIS HODGES
Pastor of Church of the Highlands
Birmingham, AL

PREFACE

A NATION DESPERATE FOR MODELS

*But in order to offer ourselves
as a model for you, so that you
would follow our example.*
—2 THESSALONIANS 3:9 NASB,
emphasis added

AMERICA IS IN trouble.

Serious trouble.

Deep trouble.

Like an eighteen-wheeler loaded to the hilt with nuclear explosives sliding down a slippery mountain pass, we're out of control. Without some drastic intervention and corrective steering, the end result is going to be catastrophic. The explosives we're loaded down with are our own sins, both individual and corporate. Immorality that would have shocked and embarrassed us years ago has become not just accepted, but *embraced* and *celebrated*. Our financial system recently came near to collapse and is currently teetering on the edge of implosion. Worst of all, our spiritual leadership seems to have lost its moorings. America has gained in affluence but has lost its influence.

I just turned sixty and have been in public ministry for over forty years. I've never seen it this bad—never. There's a passion burning inside me. My spirit is heavy, and I've wept for our country. God has laid a burden upon my heart that if something doesn't change soon, our nation will be lost.

IT WILL BE.

There *is* good news though. It's not too late. Weak though it may be, America still has a pulse. She *can* be revived! God is in the restoration business. He's restored nations in the past. He can do it again. But what has the potential to turn it around? A different president or Congress? A new Supreme Court appointment or political party? I wish it were so. I've given considerable time and energy trying to make a difference in those areas. Now, however, I'm quite convinced that the only hope for our nation lies in one of its most precious resources, its men. It's time for the Christian men to put away their toys and secret sins and lead by example. They must rise above the pack and become *model men*.

Becoming a *model man* is what this book is all about. The theme is expressed in Second Thessalonians 3:7-9:

> *You yourselves know how you ought to follow our **example**, because we did not act in an undisciplined manner among you, nor did we eat anyone's bread without paying for it, but with labor and hardship we kept working night and day so that we would not be a burden to any of you; not because we do not have the right to this, but in order to offer ourselves as a **model** for you, so that you would follow our **example**.* (2 Thessalonians 3:7-9 NASB, emphasis added)

Here Paul happens to be addressing the issue of laziness, yet there is a much deeper, broader application. Paul's entire approach to living was to do it in such a manner that qualified him as a model for others. The word translated "model" in this passage comes from the Greek term *typos,* from which we get our word *type.* It referred to a stamp or a seal that was pressed onto papyrus, forming an impression. To be a model is to make an impression. Impressions can be good or bad. Can you imagine if something in that stamp (like a notary seal or a seal at the post office) was misspelled? The result would be thousands of documents having wrong impressions. The characters on the stamp would have to be corrected in order to not continue making that mistake.

As men, we don't realize the impressions we are making upon our children, the people we work with, perhaps thousands of people around us. If one letter in our character is out of place, we are making wrong impressions on those who look to us for direction, guidance, and example. What kind of impressions are you making?

Impressions matter.

Paul understood this and knew eyes were on him watching every move he made. Without a smartphone, a computer, or even a Twitter account, Paul was a walking "model" who had so allowed God to readjust his character that he positively "impressed" thousands of lives in the first century. He sought to be a model man, one whose way of life, integrity, purity, pace, purpose, and legacy could shake a godless Roman empire. Paul also wrote in First Corinthians 4:16, *"Therefore I urge you,* **imitate** *me"* (emphasis added). He said again in First Corinthians 11:1, *"Imitate me, just as I also* **imitate** *Christ"* (NLT, emphasis added). Can you say that about yourself? Can you tell your kids and family members and coworkers to imitate you? Was Paul being arrogant? Not at all. He was a man with imperfections just like all of us. He understood more than anyone his need for God's grace in his life, but he also knew who he was and who was inside him.

America is in desperate need of "Paul-like" models and examples, men that leave godly impressions on those around them. You may be thinking, *I'm just one guy. What can I do?* Let me tell you, one man can make a huge difference. I'm reminded of my own father, Roy Stockstill, and the hundreds of thousands of people influenced by his impressions. My dad is ninety-five, was married to my mother for sixty-three years before her death, and has been in the ministry for sixty-five years. I can honestly say that he truly reflects Titus 2:7: *"Show yourself in all respects to be a **model** of good works"* (emphasis added). Watching him love God and my mom, not only in word but also in action, left impressions so profound on me that it caused a trickle-down effect. My dad built a legacy that's still growing today.

Following his example, I've been married to Melanie thirty-seven years, and we have six children. On Sundays, all of our children and their beautiful, godly spouses gather with Daddy and our grandchildren for a meal of lasagna, roast beef, soft tacos, red beans and rice, or something similar. They hang around until late in the evening at our home—napping, riding golf carts, fishing, and watching sports on television.

My greatest joy right now is to watch one of my sons pastor the same church my Dad started and pastored for twenty years and that I pastored for twenty-eight years. Dad was my coach, mentor, and cheerleader. Now I'm my son's coach, mentor, and cheerleader. Between the three of us, that's fifty combined years of leadership. The church is growing under his leadership, and I'm working on my two great desires for God: *restoring integrity* and *winning the world for Christ.*

I'm truly blessed, but it all started with my Dad's impressions.

Today more than ever, we need *model men* who stand out from the common run of humanity as men of godliness and integrity.

- Model men honor their wives.

- Model men pay their bills and keep their word.

- Model men take responsibility.

- Model men vote their conscience.

- Model men tell the truth.

- Model men function as examples for the next generation.

- Model men pray for revival.

- Model men drive in traffic jams and wait in frustrating Walmart checkout lines with a sense of being watched by others as an example.

- Model men shun pornographic filth and flirting Facebook fans.

- Model men live it before they say it.

- Model men model it before they demand it.

Friend, I don't believe you are reading this book by accident. Let God ignite a fire inside of you too. It doesn't matter what you've done or how much you feel you have failed. God can restore you personally and begin to use you right where you are to start a new legacy. You are a critical part of the solution to turning this nation around, not by partisan politics, but by grassroots guts. A model man is one who can look others in the eye with strong assurance, deep compassion, and a bright future.

Quit worrying about Washington. Change yourself. *Be* something. Show up early at work, and stay self-controlled when the lawn mower won't crank! Set a standard, and be an example. Focus on being pleasing to God and Him alone. Join the ranks of millions of great leaders who have gone before us. Be like those men who stopped tyranny by sending Hitler packing.

One pastor I met recently told me his father served as a tank driver under General Patton in World War II. At one point, they were under bombardment nonstop for *thirty-eight days.* They never changed their clothes or took a bath for *thirty-eight days.* They were covered from head to toe in mud from the battle zone for *thirty-eight days.*

My daddy was another of those millions of World War II heroes. He slept many nights on the sands of North Africa, right on the ground. He and so many others showed us what men can accomplish if they will go after it with determination.

Yes, it's time for all of us X-Box boys to become model men. It's time for pastors to quit pursuing pleasure and playing around with questionable relationships. It's time for businessmen to prefer to lose a deal than tell a lie, stretch the truth, or leave out a vital fact. It's time for fathers to get back home and put their kids first. We can whine and complain all we want about our nation, but nothing will be able to stop an army of honest, honorable, and holy men.

I understand this book is hard hitting, but I make no apologies. The hour is far too late for fluff and funniness in dealing with the men of our nation. We have precious little time left to turn an audience into an army. I'm not referring to a *militant* army, but a *model* army.

WILL YOU SIGN UP?

The first section of the book deals with *character*: integrity, purity, and example. The second section is about *consistency*: pace, discipline, and purpose. The final section is about *connection*: your marriage, your children, and your legacy.

Come on, guys! We can do this! You can do this! Be all that God envisions for you to be.

Be a model man!

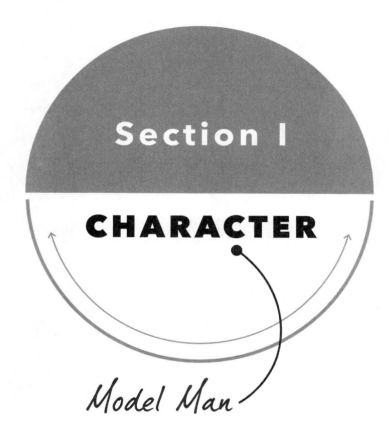

Section I

CHARACTER

Model Man

COURAGEOUS INTEGRITY

*Let integrity and uprightness preserve
me.* —PSALM 25:21, NKJV

INTEGRITY...WHAT IS IT? Simply put, integrity is the courage to do the right thing. It's living a life of uprightness in the face of a corrupt world. And let me tell you, in today's world that takes some courage. Normally, when we ponder the word courage, images instantly fill our minds of gallant soldiers flinging their bodies onto incoming RPGs in order to save their comrades, or selfless teachers taking bullets to protect innocent students during school shootings. The rescuers from 9/11 displayed dauntless courage as they sprinted into the World Trade Centers that fateful morning knowing full well the buildings were about to collapse. Those are all courageous acts indeed. Thank God for the bravery of men like that. America needs more of them. But have you considered the raw courage it takes to walk with integrity? It's not as glamorous as other heroic acts, but it's no less important. In fact, integrity is the foundation and basis of the model man.

We hear stories or see images of Christians that died as martyrs for Christ and wonder if we would ever have the courage to do that. I do believe in those moments God grants a special grace. Yet few of us realize that it also takes great courage to live uprightly for Christ day in and day out, to walk through the daily grind of this life with unswerving *integrity,* doing the right things when no one is watching, *living by standards, principles, conscience, and convictions 100 percent of the time.*

Today men are defined in many ways—by how much they can bench press, how many expensive toys they own, how much money they make or power they wield. You get it. But I maintain that a real man is defined by his integrity. Proverbs 22:1 says, *"A good name is more desirable than great riches, to be esteemed is better than silver or gold"* (NIV). How are you defined? Can you be bought, bribed, or manipulated? Does your good name mean more to you than any amount of money or compromise with sin?

The word *integrity* itself is derived from the same root as *integer,* meaning a whole number, "to be whole, no part missing." A man's character has to be whole—his thoughts, attitudes, marriage, money, and motives. Integrity is something that we are continually developing over the course of our lives and I believe one reason God had you pick this book up. You see, a man can be great in many areas, but if one area of his character is compromised, it could be his downfall. I've witnessed it time and time again—men who appeared to have rock-solid success on the outside (pastors, political leaders, businessmen, husbands with wonderful marriages and families), but somewhere along the line allowed compromise in one area and a crack was formed that weakened the integrity of their foundation. No one really noticed until suddenly there was a very public collapse of their entire structure, wounding many people. What seemingly occurred overnight, in reality, had been gradually mounting over time. Compromise is like that. It starts off small but grows stealthily until—*bam!*—it's too late. If we are going to prevent the collapse of our nation, we men must have the *courage* to walk with integrity regardless of the costs.

Everything starts with integrity.

Being a Man of Your Word

My ninety-five-year-old dad has described to me a time in our nation when men were defined by their word. Deals would be struck, money would be loaned, and property bought simply with a handshake and a promise. The idea of breaking their word was totally foreign to them. Men looked each other in the eye and were, in essence, saying, "I'd rather die than not repay this money or conclude this deal." In that day, a man's word was his bond. It was considered the highest of compliments for someone to say of you, "Now he's a man of his word." Oh God, give us men of their word today!

The Bible says that the Lord was with Samuel and *"let none of his words fall to the ground"* (1 Samuel 3:19). Samuel was a young man, but he was respected for the accuracy of his words. When you make a commitment to someone, it becomes the most important thing in your life to honor that commitment. Integrity is the making of promises and the keeping of those promises.

As a father, I learned that my children would hold me accountable for every promise I made to them. As a pastor, I learned that my church members would likewise hold me accountable for every announcement I made from the pulpit. Our motto at Bethany was, "If I said it, we have to do it." Honoring your word is godly, literally "like God." He honors His Word and His promises. So should we.

It's important to honor our word in the little things as well as the big things. If we don't honor our word in the small matters, we will surely compromise in the larger ones.

Make a habit of listening to yourself in conversations.

Did you just tell that person you would call him later today? How do you intend to remind yourself of that commitment so he is not waiting for your call until bedtime?

Did you just tell your wife you would be home at 5:00 for dinner? Will you have the discipline to be in your car after work at 4:30 to be sure you have enough time to honor her hard work in cooking for you?

Did you just tell that customer you would make it good if the product didn't work for them? Do you have the apparatus to serve that customer when they do call back, or do you just intend to become hard to find at that point?

Billy Joe Daugherty, one of my close ministry friends, was a pastor of the large Victory Christian Center in Tulsa, Oklahoma, before his death from cancer several years ago. He exemplified integrity almost as much as any man I have ever known.

When Russia opened to the gospel in the early 1990s, Billy Joe went to Saint Petersburg and committed to those who attended a Lester Sumrall crusade that he would return each month for eighteen months in a row for another huge crusade in a twenty-thousand-seat stadium. Like clockwork, he returned eighteen months in a row to preach on Friday night and Saturday morning, then flew home and preached in his pulpit on Sunday.

On one of those Russian crusades, he noticed something different about the handbill the crusade staff had passed out. Terry Henshaw, his American assistant, informed Billy Joe that they had scheduled an additional concert for the crusade, featuring an American singer on Saturday night. "Unfortunately, the singer had to cancel because of an accident," Terry said. "We have cancelled the stadium and sound system for Saturday night, but the other events of the weekend will go on as normal."

Billy Joe asked him how many handbills had been printed and passed out. When he learned it was one hundred thousand, he said, "We are going to have a concert!"

His assistant replied, "We have no singer, and the whole venue is cancelled."

"Terry," Billy Joe replied, "that line on that piece of paper is our word and our integrity. *You* are going to sing!"

Pastor Daugherty left to go back to the States that Saturday afternoon. At great expense, Terry had to re-reserve the stadium and rehire the sound system for the concert. When he eased his car around the back of the huge stadium, he didn't hear a sound inside. He thought that there was no one there.

To his surprise, when he parted the stage curtains and looked out into the arena, there were eight thousand citizens of Saint Petersburg sitting there. They had not gotten the word the concert was cancelled! Using two back-up singers, Terry sang a few songs, preached a simple message—*and three hundred people came forward to accept Christ.*

Because of integrity.

TELLING THE TRUTH

Integrity is the foundation of the model man, and truth is the foundation of integrity. Being real, authentic, genuine, and transparent builds integrity and restores it when it is broken. I have learned that people are very forgiving when I make a mistake but tend to lose confidence when they feel I am not truthful and genuine.

Have you ever wondered why a court officer asks witnesses in a trial to raise their right hand and repeat after him, "Do you promise to tell the truth, the whole truth, and nothing but the truth?" It's because we have figured out so many ways to lie!

The oath should stop after the first phrase, "Do you promise to tell the truth?" Instead, the officer must ask us if we are telling the "whole" truth because we may be withholding information that would change the judgment of a juror about someone's guilt or innocence. We call that a "half-truth." In the same way, we are asked if we are telling "nothing but" the truth because sometimes people feel the need to embellish and dramatically exaggerate the facts in order to persuade a juror.

We could define a lie, then, as *something communicated with the intent to deceive*. It is possible to say absolutely nothing and still be deceptive. If I allow others to have a favorable but wrong perception of me without telling them the facts, it is a lie. If I withhold vital information that would change someone's opinion of something, that is a lie. If I inflate the capabilities of a product or exaggerate my achievements, that is a lie.

People expect certain occupations to be disposed toward coloring the facts in order to sell a product or gain influence. In fact, America has come to be comfortable with lying. Comedian George Carlin recently joked, "The real reason that we can't have the Ten Commandments in a courthouse: You cannot post 'Thou shalt not steal,' 'Thou shalt not commit adultery,' and 'Thou shalt not lie' in a building full of lawyers, judges, and politicians. It creates a hostile work environment!" He got a big laugh, but it's really sad because it's true. Studies have shown that a high percentage of people now believe that lying is a normal part of life.[1]

May that not be true for us!

Careful, thoughtful attention to our words and the perceptions of others is how we tell the truth. And if you happen to be married, honesty should start with your wife. Even if you know that you've blown it and may be embarrassed, you must never lie to your wife. The strength of your relationship should be built on mutual trust, and that starts with telling each other the truth.

Check the accuracy of every word that comes from your mouth. Is that description you just gave of one of your achievements an accurate portrayal of what really happened? Have you noticed a tendency to elasticize events and stories so that others will be impressed? It's better to have lower numbers than to be a liar. There is no embarrassment like being labeled a liar. On the job, face up to your failures and weaknesses without blaming others or manipulating to save face. *"I blew that one."* There, you said it. Your boss thinks, "Finally, someone I can trust! I'm going to find a way to work him into a higher position of responsibility." Having had many employees through the years, I can tell you that when a man admits his mistakes to me without covering up or blaming others, I make a mental note that this is a man I can trust.

A man that is secure in who he is does not need to lie, even when he makes mistakes. Insecurity breeds lies.

Billy Graham was always the platinum standard of integrity throughout his many years of ministry. Fifty-six times he was voted as one of the world's most admired men in the Gallup Poll. It is interesting that one of the tenets of how his organization operated was to be "honest and reliable in their publicity and reporting of results."[2] To this day, you will see a number for attendance and invitation responses that are accurate *to the person* of what actually occurred. His refusal to exaggerate gave him a world platform to sit with presidents and kings.

Paying Your Bills

Your integrity must include your finances. After all, your finances tell people more about your integrity than almost any other indicator. Bad credit scores, assessments for back taxes, and mishandling of funds can be deadly to your reputation and career. The opposite is also true: if you handle money responsibly, people will respect and trust you more.

One day my assistant told me the local ABC affiliate television station had asked me to come to their station for a luncheon but hadn't said why. I had been on that station for many years with a ninety-second inspirational thought. I was the only person with Christian programming that the family who owned the station would allow to buy airtime, and they owned our local newspaper as well. They were *the* media family of Baton Rouge. When I heard about the lunch invitation, I wondered if perhaps they were going to do some negative story on our ministry!

To my surprise, the luncheon was cordial, and the station owner said, "I'm sure you are wondering why you are here. We have done a study of our entire customer base and discovered that you are our only customer who has never been late in paying his account. We just wanted to honor you."

Sigh of relief.

People in your community know you by your finances. Paying your bills on time is a big deal. The longer you do that, the higher your credit score and the higher the community's opinion of you.

America is on the precipice of financial disaster because of a free-flowing, "pay when you can" attitude toward the future. It's a shame more people aren't like my dad. He built his first house by using his paycheck on Friday to buy a few panels of Sheetrock and install them on Saturday. I have visited that little home (still standing sixty years later) and have marveled that my parents built it for *cash*. Daddy says he didn't have enough sense to know you could borrow money on a home!

Budget yourself with margins (more on this in the "Pace of Grace" chapter). Live within your means. Don't buy everything your eyes look at. The American system is based upon the pressure to buy the "last one." Daddy told me once, "I have confidence in the American mercantile system that they will always make one more."

An equal area of financial integrity is taxes. Paul said in Romans 13:6-8: *"Pay taxes, for the authorities are ministers of God, attending to this very thing. Pay to all what is owed to them: taxes to whom taxes are owed, revenue to whom revenue is owed, respect to whom respect is owed, honor to whom honor is owed. Owe no one anything, except to love each other."*

None of us wants to *over*pay the government, but our integrity demands that we *fairly* and *promptly* pay the government. We have representatives to address our taxation concerns, but that does not affect how we fill out our tax forms by April 15.

To me, the same principle holds true with God and His tithe. If I can't have integrity with God's tenth, how will I have integrity with man's obligations?

Wayne Meyers, the legendary missionary to Mexico for over sixty-five years, told of riding along with a Mexican pastor who admitted to Wayne that he didn't tithe.

"Stop the car and let me out!" Wayne said abruptly.

The pastor replied, "But sir, these roads are full of bandits."

Wayne said to the pastor, "I would rather take my chances with men who rob other men than with someone who is daring enough to rob God!"

A final area of fiscal integrity has to do with those small day-to-day decisions we make on reimbursements and company benefits. Daniel was so meticulous in his handling of finances that his enemies *"could find no ground for complaint or any fault, because he was faithful, and no error or fault was found in him"* (Daniel 6:4). Is that small fudging on an expense report really worth it if there is an investigation and your reputation is destroyed by your small, behind-the-scenes decisions on road trips?

One of my church members came to me once about a screw he had picked up from a huge barrel full of them at his workplace. He needed a screw just that size to fix an appliance at home and thought nothing about dropping it into his pocket. On the way home from work that evening, however, he passed his local hardware store and a voice spoke to him from within: "Is that little screw worth sacrificing your integrity before God and your company?" He steered his car toward the store and purchased the same screw for only pennies, returning the company's screw the next day. I know that may sound extreme, but it's not. We build habits by starting with the small things.

When our state was hit with a powerful hurricane (not Katrina) several years ago, money poured in to our church from all over America to aid the victims. Over several months, we disbursed the funds carefully, helping with roofs, supplies, and even churches that had no power.

After almost a year of benevolence, we could no longer find a legitimate need that was unmet, and we still had $25,000 in the relief account. My CFO asked me what to do with it, and I remembered that one very wealthy businessman had given exactly $25,000 into the fund. We returned his money and told him of our gratitude, saying that the project no longer required funding.

A couple of weeks later, I got a letter from this billionaire. In essence, he said, "In all my years of philanthropy, I have never had anyone return money to me. Because of this integrity, I will look forward to supporting your ministry any way I can in the future with even more resources."

———◆———

Integrity…It's the foundation of who you are, what your family will become, and how successful your business endeavors will be. It's how you behave when no one is looking. It is living your life in the fear of God without regard for man's opinion. Living with integrity takes *courage*.

Be courageous and do the right thing. It will preserve you and your family.

If you just got this one chapter, it would be worth your getting this book. We have eight more principles like this, each one shaping, molding, and making you into God's model.

DISCUSSION QUESTIONS

1. Integrity is about truth, whereas a lie is a statement made with the intent to deceive. Discuss the importance of telling the whole truth and nothing but the truth.

2. "A man's word is his bond." Verbal commitments meant more a generation ago than they do now. Give an example of a time when you had to keep your word even though it cost you something to do it.

3. Paying your bills on time seems to be unimportant...until your credit score comes out! What steps have you taken to ensure that your payments will never be late?

4. Stealing can take many forms: evading taxes, withholding tithes, removing items from your workplace, and so on. Is the Lord dealing with you about something you need to return to the government, to the Lord, to a neighbor, or to your company?

NOTES

1. For example, an Associated Press poll showed that four in ten Americans believe lying is justified sometimes. The same number believe it is all right to exaggerate a story sometimes, and a third say it's all right to lie to get a sick day. "The Associated Press Lying Study," June 28, 2006, http://surveys.ap.org/data/Ipsos/national/2006/2006-06-28%20LYING%20Study.pdf.

2. Billy Graham Center, "What part did the Modesto Manifesto play in the ministry of Billy Graham?" http://www2.wheaton.edu/bgc/archives/faq/4.htm.

THE WAR ON
SEXUAL PURITY

Whoever has no rule over his own spirit
is like a city broken down, without
walls. —**PROVERBS 25:28, NKJV**

MEN, HEAR ME. The enemy has launched a full fron-
tal attack against us. This is not some game where the
prize is a trophy, a championship ring, or even a seven-fig-
ure contract. No, the stakes are much higher. We're in a
nasty, dirty, violent war for our very souls and the souls
of our wives and children, even for our brothers in Christ.
The wounds and casualties of this conflict are just as real
as the ones in Iraq, Vietnam, or any other war. Satan's not
messing around. He plays for keeps, and he's out to steal,
kill, and destroy everything we hold dear—everything.
Satan knows if he can bring us down, he can bring down
our families, our churches, and ultimately our nation.

We have an enemy that is set on our destruction.

Nehemiah 4:14 urges us, *"Do not be afraid....Remember the Lord, who is great and awesome, and fight for your brothers, your sons and your daughters, your wives and your homes."*

Are you willing to stand your ground and fight for what's important? To be a *model man*, you're going to have to fight.

In this war, the enemy has many weapons, but his weapon of choice against men is sexual impurity. Since the beginning of time, Satan has been using lust and perverted sexuality to wreck men's lives and effectiveness, but it seems in these last days he's taken his attacks on purity to nuclear levels. No one actually expects moral purity anymore. To most, even the thought of sexual purity is ridiculous. Still, the media pounces like ravenous wolves upon men in the public eye who have fallen because they could not control themselves sexually. Just in the last few years, the stories of unfaithful pastors, four-star generals, leading congressmen, governors, and philandering athletes have dominated our news. Their relationships, reputations, and futures were ruined by a lack of self-control.

While I was writing this chapter, a prominent pastor of a 20,000-plus member church had to step down from the pulpit for sexual misconduct. He announced to his congregation that he had succumbed to an affair, but when the whole truth came out, it was discovered that he'd had multiple affairs over the course of his ministry. We act shocked when we see such headlines, yet the truth is, we're really not that shocked at all these days. Here's why. A recent study revealed that 57 percent of married men, *Christians* included, admitted to being unfaithful, and 74 percent said they would have an affair if they would never get caught![1] What's going on in our leadership is only a reflection of what is happening in our society. Most men just feel lucky they're not in the public eye!

Something is wrong—dreadfully wrong.

The most vile, detestable type of pornography is now available at the click of a mouse. Consider the enemy's strategy with porn. Men are addicted, and it's robbing them of their precious time, productivity, and divine destinies. Satan's lies are destroying the best of their creative minds, distracting their focus, and reducing them to mere slaves. The statistics are staggering. Another study, this one by Nielson, showed that over 50 percent of *Christian* men say they are addicted to porn—not just viewing it, but addicted! Fifty-one percent of *pastors* admit that pornography is a personal temptation, and 40 percent say they are struggling with it. One third of those 40 percent say they have looked at porn in the last month.[2]

In America, over 2 million dollars is spent on porn every second.[3] Every second! Let that sink in for a moment. Pornography almost always leads to other sexual sins and the devaluation of spouses and families. It hinders a man's ability to hear from God. Our addiction to pornography is out of control and is a symptom of a much deeper problem. Sociologist Dr. Jill Manning said, "Research reveals many systemic effects of pornography that are undermining an already vulnerable culture of marriage and family. Even more disturbing is the fact that the first Internet generations have not reached full maturity, so the upper limits of this impact have yet to be realized."[4]

MEN, WAKE UP!

Listen to this scripture: *"For the desires of the flesh are against the Spirit, and the desires of the Spirit are against the flesh, for these are opposed to each other, **to keep you from doing the things you want to do**"* (Galatians 5:17, emphasis added). The enemy uses our flesh to keep us from doing the things that we are supposed to do—those things God is calling us to do, the things that deep down every man really wants to do. C. S. Lewis said in reference to sexuality and the flesh, "For 'nature' (in the sense of natural desire) will have to be controlled anyway, unless you are going to ruin your whole life."[5] Men are literally ruining their whole lives because of a lack of self-control. I would also add that men's lack of self-control is ruining our whole nation!

Your flesh is in a war with its cravings and its fantasies. But you don't have to put up with it.

You don't have to settle.

You can fight and you can win! A man *can* walk clean physically and mentally, committed to one wife in loyalty for life. I've witnessed it in my Dad and in other men of God. I've experienced it personally. Yes, a man can walk pure, but it won't happen by accident. If you are serious about winning this fight, you are going to have to develop some boundaries and erect some walls to keep the enemy out.

WALLS OF WAR

The scripture at the beginning of this chapter, Proverbs 25:28 says, *"Whoever has no rule over his own spirit is like a city broken down, without walls"* (NKJV). In ancient days, cities were defined by their walls. Walls actually made a statement to the inhabitants and to the enemies outside the walls. They served for protection against military aggression and gave the inhabitants great security. Simply put, if the walls of a city were broken down for any reason—neglect, fire, weather, or military siege—an enemy could just waltz in and wreak havoc. When an enemy was inside the city walls, the battle was much harder to fight.

Walls were important.

Nehemiah understood this. That's why he was so undone that the walls of Jerusalem had been broken down (Nehemiah 1:3). He was so grieved that he cried out to God. *"So it was, when I heard these words, that I sat down and wept, and mourned for many days; I was fasting and praying before the God of heaven"* (Nehemiah 1:4, NKJV). Soon afterwards, God called Nehemiah to the important task of rebuilding the walls.

How about the city of your life? Do have holy walls surrounding you and your family, walls that define you? Are you sending a message to the inhabitants of your circle that you are safe, that they are safe and can trust you, and for the enemy to keep his distance? Do you have towers erected, keeping a watchful eye on the tactics of your opponent? Or are your walls broken down, allowing the enemy to come in and wreak havoc?

Men with broken-down walls are trying to fight the enemy when he's too close. God is calling men to rebuild the walls and create safe boundaries in their lives. This kind of radical action is what it is going to take to defeat the enemy of sexual impurity. Walls are boundaries that announce to the enemy, "You can do what you want in the world out there, but this area here is my responsibility and belongs to the Lord. You're not coming in here! I'm walled off."

Living a life without self-control or predetermined boundaries is like trying to defend a city with no walls. To win the war of purity, you've got to build a fortress around yourself. We need men like Nehemiah who are grieved, who weep and mourn because of broken-down walls, and who then get to work rebuilding!

A friend of mine lived in the country. His mother carried around a flyswatter everywhere she went inside her house to kill flies. The problem was that *she didn't have any screens on her windows!* Her son persuaded her to put screens on the windows, and guess what? Soon she no longer needed her flyswatter! Are you swatting desperately at sexual flies, but you have no screens up?

A Lesson from Samson

What a powerful leader Samson was! He was a legend. He killed a thousand men with the jawbone of a donkey. He ruled Israel for twenty years.

When Samson was born, the angel of the Lord told his parents that he was to be a Nazarite from birth (Judges 13:5). The Nazarites had only three rules they were required to follow (Numbers 6:3-60):

1. Never touch a grape or drink wine.

2. Never touch a dead body.

3. Never cut your hair.

Sounds simple, doesn't it? Following these three foundational rules kept Samson pure for most of a lifetime. Unfortunately, throughout his years of leadership, small compromises crept into his life.

First, we see him going into a vineyard and killing a lion (Judges 14:5-6). My first question to Samson in that situation would have been, "If you are never supposed to touch a grape, what are you doing in a vineyard?"

Second, we see him going back to the vineyard sometime later and putting his hand in the carcass of the lion to gather honey (Judges 14:8). My second question to Samson is, "If you are never supposed to touch a dead body, what are you doing touching a lion carcass?"

By breaking these first two rules of behavior, it was easy for him to lay his head in the lap of a prostitute and get his first haircut.

It seems to me that if you can keep a few standards for your whole lifetime, your chances of remaining sexually faithful to your wife are almost 100 percent. *Those standards stand like walls around your mind and heart, protecting you from the sexual attacks that are sure to come.* We'll be getting to them in this chapter.

PURITY, BILLY GRAHAM STYLE

In the integrity chapter we just read, I mentioned Billy Graham as the platinum standard of marital fidelity and sexual purity. Within the same agreement called the "Modesto Manifesto" was a standard that the Graham ministry has used now for over sixty-five years: "Never be alone with a woman." It's a standard any of us could adopt.

The power of that guideline is that you never put yourself in a position to be tempted to engage in intimacy with any woman other than your wife. In addition, it means that no woman would ever be able to falsely accuse you of making advances toward her in a private setting with no other witnesses.

I was privileged to interview Dr. Tom Phillips, vice president of the Billy Graham Library. He confirmed to me that he searched Dr. Graham's hotel room at night (closet, bathroom, under the beds) to be certain no one else was in the room before Dr. Graham retired for the night. One of Dr. Graham's associate evangelists rented the room directly across the hall from him so that he could observe anyone coming or going through Dr. Graham's door.

Such guidelines may seem archaic and foolish in today's society, but look at the fruit of keeping a few small standards faithfully for life: a life with a happy marriage and a reputation that remains unspotted and unsoiled.

DAVID'S WORST NIGHTMARE

Success followed everything David did. He won every battle, killed every giant, and conquered every opposing nation. He even outlived his early enemy, Saul, who chased him for years through the Judaean countryside.

One night, however, his guard was down. From the rooftop of his palace, his eyes caught the form of a woman bathing without quite enough curtains in place. He didn't know who she was, but her form enticed him, and he fantasized about sexual contact with her. When he sent for her, he found out to his surprise that she was the wife of one of the top lieutenants in his army. The rest is history.

I was watching the amazing BBC television special called *Planet Earth* several years ago. The fourth episode, titled "Caves," told about a deep cave in New Zealand.

When the camera crew reached the inky blackness of the bottom of the cave, they saw thousands of blinking lights on the roof of the cave. These blinking lights came from the New Zealand glowworm and appeared almost like stars on the roof of the cave. Hanging under each light was a strand of silk, about eighteen inches long, that the glowworm carefully made from a very sticky substance. From the bottom of the cave, moths were attracted by the blinking lights and curiously made their way to the ceiling to investigate. What they didn't know was that the silk that hung almost invisible in the darkness would stick to their wings the moment they touched it and was impossible to be released from.

As I watched this documentary, I saw one moth's wing become stuck. The moth flew around in a circle, trying to get free. But then its other wing became stuck. Next, the moth's abdomen attached to the silk, and I could see it writhing wildly as it was suspended in midair.

Now the glowworm began to retract the silk. Higher and higher, toward the glowworm's mouth, the helpless and exhausted moth was raised. Finally, I heard the *crunch* as the worm slowly ate the moth until it disappeared.

The Lord said to me in that moment: "That is what is happening to My servants. They become curious at something attractive. They leave the security of their home and make an advance toward the 'blinking light.' Little do they realize that they are becoming attached with every look, every text, every visit, every touch, and every embrace."

Proverbs 7:22-23 says, *"Immediately he went after her, as an ox goes to the slaughter, or as a fool to the correction of the stocks, till an arrow struck his liver. As a bird hastens to the snare, he did not know it would cost his life"* (NKJV).

Satan's plan is to *"steal and kill and destroy"* (John 10:10). He even turns simple curiosity into a catastrophe.

Personal Guidelines

You *must* have personal guidelines set up in order to remain sexually pure. If you drift from day to day, situation to situation, without nonnegotiables, you can find yourself over the line where it is difficult to return.

Niagara Falls has a sign at a certain point warning that no rescue effort is possible if you pass this point, because you will surely be swept over the falls by the mighty current. There's a similar kind of danger point in sexual temptation. Stay far away from that line! Don't flirt with the danger of an illicit relationship. You don't have the strength and power to overcome once you reach a certain stage. Instead, stick to the following guidelines of accountability, compatibility, and reliability.

1. Accountability

Someone told me once, "We all do better when we are watched." Accountability simply means that we are voluntarily putting ourselves in a position where others can watch over our souls. It is nearly impossible to fall into an affair, an illicit relationship, or a pornographic habit if you keep yourself within eyesight of others.

Practically speaking, this means that we openly and willingly inform our spouse of our whereabouts and relationships. My wife knows *where* I am and *who* I am with all day, every day. I travel frequently around the city, but she knows my schedule and route. I don't turn up a half hour away from where I told her I was to be. If something causes me to change my plans, I call and let her know.

"What about freedom?" you may say.

My response is that a train is free only when it is on the tracks.

Travel with a partner.

Of course, there will be times when you cannot have another person with you, but it is then that you are most vulnerable. Jesus sent His team out two by two for a reason (Luke 10:1). I have brought my children, other pastors, and my wife on many international trips for the sole purpose of providing safety and accountability. I tell the group inviting me that I prefer two tickets rather than an honorarium. I'm very serious about the Paul-and-Silas approach.

Filter the Internet.

Your IT director (or wife) can install a filter on any Internet device and be the administrator of that filter. Of course, any technical system can be defeated, but 99 percent of random, accidental pornography exposures will be eliminated if you install filtering software. With the insidious pornography industry constantly trying to put an image in front of your eyes through e-mail, Twitter, text, and web cookies, you *must* put up protection!

I realize that at times a filter will mistakenly stop a legitimate site you want to look at. It's not a big deal. Remember that you didn't even have the Internet until Al Gore invented it!

Control your cable.

Some cable programming turns into hard-core pornography after eleven o'clock each night. Your cable company allows you to block these networks. Remember, there are five hundred cable channels. Surely you can do without a handful that show their enticing images to you when you are tired and vulnerable.

I checked into a hotel several years ago, and the moment I turned on the TV set, a pornographic movie flashed in my face. I turned the set off and complained to the manager, who promptly blocked all pornographic channels to my room.

We are in a battle!

Monitor your mail.

Even the mail system has become a channel for soft porn to be delivered right to your door. After receiving a risqué magazine advertisement, my wife and I visited the post office with what they had delivered to our home. They apologized and told us we could have our name placed on a list blocking any such material. We did, they did, and it was over.

Watch your workplace.

In today's world, men are often thrown into work situations in close proximity with women on the team. Unfortunately, there are occasionally a few women there whose home lives are deplorable and who long for intimacy. Maintain the rules of never being alone, even discussing it with a supervisor if you feel uncomfortable in those environments. Of course, *never touch!* A touch leads to a kiss, a kiss to an embrace, an embrace to a full-blown affair.

2. Compatibility

"The best defense is a good offense." (That's not in the Bible, but it could be!) If your marriage relationship is deep and intimate, you will have almost zero desire for another woman. (I will deal with this subject more fully in the seventh chapter, on marriage.) When you lose your attraction to your wife, when your schedules turn you into ships passing in the harbor, when stress and fatigue wear down your defenses, you are a prime candidate for a secret relationship.

Maintain a healthy sex life.

Paul warned of the dangers of a couple's sex life becoming sporadic and seasonal: *"Do not deprive one another, except perhaps by agreement for a limited time, that you may devote yourselves to prayer; but then come together again, so that Satan may not tempt you because of your lack of self-control"* (First Corinthians 7:5).

In other words, your sexual relationship and contact should be regular, romantic, and rewarding. Satan is waiting to probe through a crack in the wall where either of you no longer feels an attraction to the other or begins to fantasize about an intimate relationship with someone else.

If you have lost attraction to your spouse, seek counseling. You may have a physical, emotional, or psychological block that is causing you to lose interest in each other.

Reconnect romantically.

Evenings should be shared because it is prime time for the two of you to watch a short movie or television series that you both enjoy after the kids are in bed. Let your nighttime routine be conducive to fun, intimate fellowship before retiring. Get in bed at a decent hour—with the phone unplugged! These small steps can save your marriage and prevent the destruction of your spiritual model.

Guard your wife.

Be sensitive to the emotional state and challenges your wife is going through. Never put her in a position where she could be tempted by another man—a maintenance man, a houseguest, or whoever he might be. If your relationship is at a low state, she might be tempted by an advance from another man, something that could be equally as devastating as *you* being tripped up by the enemy.

3. Reliability

Accountability is the first stage of purity that guards you from danger. Compatibility is the second stage, causing moral temptations to be almost trivial and foolish. The final nonnegotiable you need in order to remain pure your entire life is a system of reliable, consistent relationships and activities that you never miss. Without these systems in place, you become inconsistent and more vulnerable to mood swings, holiday temptations, and low points where your weaknesses take hold of your intentions.

The book of Ecclesiastes tells us, *"Two are better than one, because they have a good reward for their toil. For if they fall, one will lift up his fellow. But woe to him who is alone when he falls and has not another to lift him up!"* (Ecclesiastes 4:9-10). We need other people.

Here are a few systems that I have in place to maintain reliable relationships and that I recommend to you:

Participate in a weekly small group.

I believe in the importance of a weekly time in a church service where worship and preaching lift me and encourage me (Hebrews 10:25). But I have learned, in addition, that a weekly small group with other men who battle the same temptations I do has tremendous power to keep me pure. John Wesley had sixty thousand Methodist believers in weekly small groups in England, held together by a simple question each member answered in turn: "What temptation did you face this week, and how did you overcome it?"

If you are looking, not at the backs of the heads of people in church, but into the faces of the men in your small group every week, you are in the ideal situation to be transparent, real, and vulnerable. Jesus said, *"Where two or three are gathered in my name, there am I among them"* (Matthew 18:20). This book will be followed up by a separate series of small-group lessons that will help you begin a group for men in your church that you will surely be strengthened by.

Each week in our church, about two hundred businessmen sit around twenty-four tables of eight chairs each and talk through a short lesson in a one-hour meeting of a meal (twenty minutes), a lesson (twenty minutes), and a discussion/prayer time (twenty minutes). It's simple. It's short. There's nothing magical about it, but it is a *system* that strengthens even the weakest Christian who attends to become a lion for God. (More about this in the conclusion.)

Stick to a daily Bible reading plan.

Since 1990, our church has read through the *One Year Bible* reading plan, which leads you through the entire Bible in about fifty minutes a day.

Jesus said, *"Sanctify them in the truth; your word is truth"* (John 17:17). We've got multiple translations in our bookcases and the YouVersion app on our iPhones. The problem is not in *having* Bibles, but in *using* Bibles. If a man—any man—will commit to consistency in a daily Bible reading plan, his spiritual maturity will go through the roof and his vulnerability to temptation will become insignificant.

Daily reading of the Scripture is like putting up screens to keep out the flies of temptation. It is your strongest defense against infiltration by Satan in the sexual area.

Practice prayer and fasting.

Luke 4:3-13 and First John 2:16 show us that Jesus went through forty days of prayer and fasting to strengthen Himself against the three greatest temptations of His life-time: the lust of the flesh (bread), the lust of the eyes (power), and the pride of life (the temple). Why would the same thing not work for us?

Throughout my years as a Christian, I have learned the power of daily prayer and weekly fasting. My prayer time may be a few minutes or up to an hour. I have tried to fast at least one day a week until supper time (usually Saturday). Something about that simple routine has empowered me to have a spiritual edge against temptation. It has reconnected my spirit with the Holy Spirit. Someone said, *"The purpose of the Holy Spirit is to make a holy spirit"* (within you!).

You can do this thing! If you will make yourself accountable to others, draw closer to your spouse, and maintain systems of spiritual strength every week, you *are* going to make it!

Perhaps your first thought is, *I have already failed morally. I've been looking at pornography. I have made advances toward other women. Is there any hope this cycle can be broken and my life become a fortress of strength, stability, and purity?*

The answer is yes. There is hope.

Find some spiritual brothers who can help. As Paul says, *"Brothers, if anyone is caught in any transgression, you who are spiritual should restore him in a spirit of gentleness. Keep watch on yourself, lest you too be tempted. Bear one another's burdens, and so fulfill the law of Christ"* (Galatians 6:1-2). Pour out your soul. Get real, honest, and transparent. Open the windows of your soul to the light. Renounce (with your brothers) every wrong thought, relationship, and past action. Come to the cross of Christ and let His blood wash away the past failures. Invite the Holy Spirit to fill you with strength.

Congratulations! You have just made it through the most difficult area for men to conquer. God is already restoring your *integrity*, and now He is restoring your *purity.* The third area of character in the model man is being an example.

DISCUSSION QUESTIONS

1. How do your walls and boundaries define you? Are there any areas where your walls are broken down? What steps are you taking to rebuild?

2. If Samson had kept his three little rules, he would have ruled Israel his entire life instead of dying with the Philistines. What standards have you used to keep yourself pure?

3. Billy Graham's number-one rule was "Never be alone with a woman." What situations do you face where you will have to apply that rule to your life?

4. Accountability with the Internet, your travel, cable TV, and your workplace is critical. What systems have you put in place to be sure temptation cannot overcome you in one of these areas?

5. If you are married, sexual compatibility with your wife can stop a lot of temptation. Discuss the challenge it is to maintain sexual intimacy in this fast-paced and high-pressured world.

NOTES

1. Mark Laaser, MDiv, PhD, *The Fight of Your Life* (©2014 FOYL Events), 5, www.infidelityfacts.com.

2. Mark Laaser, MDiv, PhD, *The Fight of Your Life* (©2014 FOYL Events), 2, www.covenanteyes.com.

3. United Families International Blog, *Huffington Post*.

4. Dr. Jill Manning, *Pornography's Impact on Marriage & The Family*, The Heritage Foundation, Nov. 9, 2005, http://www.heritage.org/research/testimony/pornographys-impact-on-marriage-amp-the-family.

5. C. S. Lewis, *Mere Christianity* (New York: Simon & Schuster Inc. Touchstone, Ed. 1980), 94.

CHAPTER 3

ALL EYES ARE ON YOU

But set the believers an example in speech,
in conduct, in love, in faith, in purity.
—1 TIMOTHY 4:12, emphasis added

THE THIRD CRITICAL element of a *model man's* character is being an *example*. *Integrity* is what we are like before God when nobody is looking. *Purity* is having strong boundaries and walls around us guarding our hearts from sexual immorality. *Example* is how we are perceived by others in our circle of influence. Like a three-legged stool, if one leg is missing, our character cannot stand, nor will it hold up under pressure. It takes all three legs to be properly balanced and strong.

Most of us have at one time or another been disappointed by those who are set up as role models in our nation. It seems almost daily we hear of another high-profile athlete being arrested on charges ranging anywhere from illegal drugs to robbery to rape. Routinely, some politician or pastor is smeared across the news after being caught cheating on their spouse or being involved in another financial scandal. Entertainers are coming out of the closet left and right, arrogantly flaunting their sin in front of the cameras, while the so-called straight stars hop from bed to bed with little or no standard of morality. These types crave the limelight, but shun the spotlight, refusing to take responsibility for being role models.

As a *model man*, you may not be in the limelight, but you *do* have eyes on you. Someone *is* watching every move you make. Even if it is only one person, that one person is just as important as one million. You see, God is all about the ones. He's about using us to reach the individuals that come into our circle of influence over the course of our lives.

One Sunday a pastor of one of the larger, more dynamic churches in Baton Rouge took a "show of hands" survey of his congregation. He asked how many of them had come to know the Lord through an evangelist or television ministry. A few hands speckled across the sanctuary. Next, he asked how many had come to the Lord as a result of being witnessed to by a stranger. Again, a few hands went up. Finally, he asked how many had come to the Lord because they were influenced by a friend or family member. A sea of hands shot into the air, almost the whole church! God uses all these different methods to plant seeds and draw people to Himself, but most of the time it is the influence of a personal relationship that God uses to close the deal and bring lasting discipleship.

For those of us who sometimes feel small and insignificant, our success as *model men* is not in our size, but in our stature; not in our results, but in our reputation. Never downplay the importance of reaching one person. As Mother Teresa moved quietly from bed to bed in a Calcutta ward for the incurable, she surely never dreamed that the world would one day look at her photo and be inspired. Those you are working alongside or leading *right now* could be drawing life lessons that will propel them far beyond your own success.

In order to bring our nation back to righteousness, it must be filled with men who accept the responsibility of being looked up to wherever they are in life. They are not afraid of close inspection. Though certainly not perfect, they strive to do nothing that offends, misleads, or disappoints the next generation. When they mess up, they are quick to admit it and seek forgiveness. Often the very act of admitting we were wrong and seeking forgiveness models to others the grace of God in action. Whether he's a coach, teacher, businessman, husband, father, or pipe fitter, the *model man* thinks in terms of how a lost world perceives him as a Christian witness.

Paul challenges us:

> *Brothers, join in imitating me, and keep your eyes on those who walk according to the* **example** *you have in us* (Philippians 3:17, emphasis added).

> *Let no one despise you for your youth, but set the believers an* **example** *in speech, in conduct, in love, in faith, in purity* (1 Timothy 4:12, emphasis added).

How about you? Are you setting an example for other believers to follow as well as for unbelievers who will judge Christianity by what they see in you? Can you stand the scrutiny? Are you up to the challenge? Are you ready for God to mold you, squash you, pull you, stretch you, and form you into the image of Jesus for a confused community to observe? Let's go!

OUR SPEECH

In the above passage, when Paul addresses the areas that are critical to being an effective example, he cuts to the chase and gets down to the nitty-gritty of everyday life. He begins with something incredibly practical, our *speech.* It sounds so simple and unspectacular, but let's face it, controlling the tongue is not an easy thing to do! Paul starts with speech because if we can learn to control our tongue, everything else falls in place. James 3:2 says, *"For we all stumble in many things. If anyone does not stumble in **word**, he is a perfect man, able also to bridle the whole body* (NKJV, emphasis added). Did you get that?

Control the tongue and you control the body.

It's one thing to read about controlling the tongue in this book; it's another thing to be stuck in a line of twenty people at Walmart and feel like speaking your mind. I don't know about you, but every line I get in becomes the longest line. Inevitably, there is a person at the register counting out coupons. Every other line is moving except ours. I am a busy person and really want to walk up to the register and exclaim, "Can't you see that there are twenty people in this line and we are all busy people?" The problem, however, is that I am a fairly public figure in our city, and immediately someone in the line would recognize me. Inwardly, they would think, *What's his problem? He can't control himself to wait? I thought Christianity was about peace and patience. We are all waiting patiently—why can't he?*

James continues, *"But no man can tame the tongue. It is an unruly evil, full of deadly poison* (James 3:8, NKJV). The words you speak to your wife, your children, your employees, or even fellow shoppers in a Walmart line become the measure of your spirituality to many people. Your tongue has within itself the power to speak life or death. *"Death and life are in the power of the tongue"* (Proverbs 18:21, NKJV).

One man bought a used lawn mower. The seller reminded him that it was a *used* mower and that at times it would be hard to crank. He even implied that it would, at times, "make you cuss."

The buyer, a pastor, was offended and said, "I forgot all the curse words I knew twenty-five years ago when I entered the ministry."

The seller responded, "Oh, this lawn mower will make them all come back to you!"

A kind, gracious tongue, instead of a biting, harsh, even wounding tongue, is not easy to maintain. The pressures of work, weather, worries, and screaming children can force an angry word out of almost anyone! Yes, *"no man can tame the tongue,"* only the Holy Spirit. Ask God for help to walk in the Spirit and have self-control over your tongue.

I remember a moment of truth for my family. With six children, we drove a big, fifteen-passenger van for a number of years. One day, as we drove down the traffic lane at the local mall, several teenaged young men had blocked the lane with their car as several others hung in their windows to chat. We sat for several seconds as they casually glanced at us sitting in the van and waiting on them. After thirty seconds, it became apparent that they were not leaving on purpose.

"Get out and tell them what you think, Dad!" my boys began to yell at me.

It was tempting to take the advice. But instead I quietly prayed under my breath for grace to wait the teens out. Finally, after about sixty seconds (which seemed like ten minutes!), they moved aside and glared at us as we rode past.

I'm sure you know what it's like to be in a situation where your tongue wrestles inside your mouth to get loose and say what it wants to. The next time you are about to verbally let someone have it, repeat to yourself: "I am an example."

Our Conduct

After exhorting us to set an example in speech in First Timothy 4:12, Paul then moves to the importance of our conduct.

Let's say by the time you finally make it out of that long line at Walmart, you're now really behind schedule. You go to the parking lot with your shopping basket, quickly unload it, and look for the place where you're supposed to place it. Unfortunately, the cart rack is twenty yards away. Will you do what most shoppers do? Shove their basket with their foot so that it rolls across the parking lot. I've always wanted to do that! Instead, though, I make a decision to walk my basket across the parking lot and put it into the place where it is supposed to go. Why? These actions may seem petty and small, but you never know who's watching, and trust me, they're watching! Good conduct is not only about not doing certain things. It's about behaving properly and in order.

Order is godly. Paul says, *"God is not a God of confusion…. All things should be done decently and in order"* (First Corinthians 14:33, 40). If those baskets are not put into a proper place, they will be scattered all across the parking lot, the parking spaces will be blocked, people will dangerously swerve to avoid them, and all types of chaos can happen.

The people of Israel came out of Egypt as a ragtag group of slaves. When they left Mount Sinai, they were a mighty army with banners. God put them into configuration around the ark of the covenant with three tribes each on the north, south, east, and west. They moved in order.

Satan promotes chaos, anarchy, and confusion. His kingdom thrives on terror, waste, poverty, and collapse. Jesus, by contrast, came to restore peace, order, and productivity to the world. Before He fed the five thousand, *"they sat down in groups, by hundreds and by fifties"* (Mark 6:40). Jesus would not do a miracle before there was order. In a calm, relaxed way, He fed each person and then picked up every piece of excess bread and fish, enough to fill twelve huge baskets.

This is *order*. This word teaches you how to be a great example for the Lord in every phase of your life. With the parking-lot shopping basket, I am following the guidelines and policies laid down by the retail business to maintain order and prevent injury. Likewise, I am confronted with regulations, rules, and policies everywhere I go. They maintain order in law, business, traffic, finance, marriage, education, athletics, and practically every area of life.

Something in me wants to discard these policies. I want to disregard them to show my independence. I may be tired that day and think these small rules don't really matter. *I didn't make these rules, and I'm surely not going to keep them,* I think. This defiant, rebellious attitude, if I give in to it, will destroy my example. I will set an example of mocking authority from morning until night. I will continually pay fines, break down, lose jobs, lose privileges, lose properties, lose valuables, and even lose a family over the disorder in my life.

When Jesus comes into your life, your conduct changes. You become interested in the policies of the community. The rebellious, defiant spirit is gone, and you no longer illegally pull into handicap parking spots like a

VIP. Your driving on the interstate changes so that you no longer swerve from lane to lane, flashing your lights and blowing your horn, shaking your fist and scowling at everyone else on the road. You realize that going 85 miles per hour in a 65 miles per hour zone could cause an embarrassing time of "fellowship" with an officer on the side of the road as well as a suspended license or a night in jail. You become concerned about the example you set for others and your family, even in the small things. It's not just about following rules. It's about respecting the order that promotes freedom within set boundaries.

This order in your conduct affects your living environment as well. The grass in your backyard used to be so high that you lost two children in there last year! Now you like for your yard to appear neat, trimmed, and presentable. Your garage used to look like a landfill, so that you could not open the door for fear of an avalanche! Now your tools are hanging in order on the wall, the floor is clear, and even the screws and nails are organized. Junk is cleared out of closets, unworn clothes are given to the needy, and shelves and spaces are efficiently used.

Order also affects your finances. I have been in homes where bills were piled all over a desk with no sense of what was owed and what was paid, not because of a lack of income, but because of disorder. No wonder these people missed payments. No wonder their credit ratings went down. No wonder it seemed that no matter how much money they earned, they never had enough.

One person jokingly told me, "I know I still have money in my account because I still have checks in my checkbook." That's not quite the way it works.

When your life is in order, it will change your time management as well. Punctuality is often a matter of being able to locate items before you leave for an appointment. People whose clothes are unfolded have to search for ten precious minutes for a matching sock. Then they discover their shirt is not ironed. When they finally assemble their wardrobe, they cannot find where they laid their keys. The chaos of their closet, the mess in their dresser, and their gas tank on empty causes them to be late for their appointments.

When a person is consistently late, people get the picture that their life is out of order. They will not be called upon to lead and direct in key positions, because someone will point out that their leadership will be chaotic and hard to predict.

Start with the basics. Clean out your environment. Establish a place for everything. Pay bills the day they arrive (online services makes this easy now). Leave in enough time to arrive at appointments fifteen minutes early. Plan your day the night before, your week the Sunday night before, your month in the month before, and so on. Refuse to contribute one ounce of confusion to Satan's disorder campaign.

Take pride in your appearance. You don't have to lead the world in *fashion,* but you do have to provide an example to the world in *function.* Your clothes can be neat, well matched, and functional. If you have a car, it should be well maintained and clean. You don't have to be obsessive with these things, only aware of the impact they have on those who observe your example in life.

OUR SPOUSE

The third area of being an example that Paul spoke about in First Timothy 4:12 is *your love.* Though I will devote the final third of this book to your relationships, I would like to address the key areas of marriage and parenting in this chapter in terms of your example.

Keep in mind that the family is God's model of the kingdom of God. He established a divine order in First Corinthians 11:3: *"I want you to understand that the head of every man is Christ, the head of a wife is her husband, and the head of Christ is God."*

"Head" means authority. Christ looks to God the Father as His authority, even though He is equal with God. He has every right to chart His own agenda but instead chooses voluntarily to follow the agenda of the

Father. The man, in turn, looks to Christ as his authority, even though the Bible calls us *"fellow heirs with Christ"* (Romans 8:17). The principle is that "head" does not mean a superior, but rather a leader of equals.

This principle applies, then, to a husband and his wife. They are considered equal in the sight of God, fellow heirs in the grace of life (see 1 Peter 3:7). For the purposes of order, however, she follows his lead. In the US military, each soldier is equal under the Constitution as a citizen. However, they have chosen to submit to each other on the battlefield for the purpose of order. That's the way it is in marriage.

The husband should be the provider, priest, and protector of his family (more on this in chapter 7). He is obligated to love, protect, and even give his life, if necessary, for his wife and children. His love for them causes him to put them ahead of himself, his ego, his narcissistic self-interest, and his hobbies. He lives for them.

The husband's model, then, is Christ. *"Husbands, love your wives, as Christ loved the church and gave himself up for her"* (Ephesians 5:25). He joyfully provides for her the best he can afford. He takes the lead spiritually in guiding his family to the house of God. He is ever vigilant to protect her from any awkward or dangerous situation she encounters.

He values her advice, input, and wisdom on every decision, but in the end he makes the final decision based on prayer and leads by example. She honors and follows. Most wives I know actually are begging for their husbands to make decisions!

Be affectionate with your wife. Establish routines with your wife. Do everything with your wife. Genesis 2:24 declares you are *"one flesh."* Act like it. In a day when most husbands are running around doing their own thing, be a *model* of a fun, giving, serving, fulfilling partner.

I watched my dad's model with my mother for the sixty-three years they were married before her death. They laughed, they built a mighty church, they hosted others, they sacrificed for us, and they grew old together. When Mother was in her early eighties, the symptoms of Alzheimer's became apparent. Her primary caregiver was her partner and lover of sixty years: my dad. As her symptoms worsened and she could hardly remember anyone, I saw them sitting on their loveseat kissing only two weeks before she went to heaven.

That's what I'm talking about: a loving, faithful lifestyle with your favorite person on earth that demonstrates to the whole community what it means to serve, forgive, and give yourself to another person.

Our Children

Equal to the model of your marriage is the model of your children (much more about this in chapter 8). *"Wisdom is proved right by all her children"* (Luke 7:35, NIV).

How your children behave themselves, obey, and respect authority is also a *model*. They are a direct reflection of you. (Scary thought, isn't it?) Ultimately, children do have their own free will. Still, people honor you for their accomplishments and blame you for their failures.

Children NEED models.

When I was a young boy in elementary school, I played basketball. Our coach made a habit of smoking cigarettes during practice. He would keep the cigarette in his mouth while he spoke to us, and it would bob up and down in his mouth the entire time he was speaking. When my parents at home would ask me about anything to do with basketball games, schedules, uniforms, or practices, immediately I would hold my mouth with my lips pursed together as if I were holding a cigarette in my lips!

I heard of one Bible college professor who was a great speaker. When he was especially profound, he would sling his long hair back, flipping it over his shoulder. Years later, his students could be seen doing the same thing as they spoke. Even one who became bald would sling his head back when he felt especially eloquent!

In many nations, children who are destined to become emperors and royalty are carefully groomed from an early age. Intense training is focused on their manners, cleanliness, speech, and conduct. The guardians and teachers realize that this development is critical since one day that child may lead the entire nation. In contrast, I am amazed at how haphazard and unattended many children are. They are not being groomed for anything.

Your example is grooming your children for their future.

Even your children's view of God the Father is influenced by their view of you. Many adults have a distorted view of God because their earthly fathers were poor examples of love and discipline. Many fathers have no idea where their children are or who they are with. The daily schedule and routine of their household are chaotic and haphazard. Their family is sort of like snow skiing—downhill and out of control. I recall a recent trip to a restaurant where I observed a two-year-old literally controlling the entire restaurant as his parents sat by, looking wide-eyed and unable to do anything about his tantrums and behavior!

Don't be afraid to discipline your children. Groom them carefully for big jobs and responsibilities in their future. Look at them as a direct reflection of your focus, coaching, and affirmation. Pay close attention to their feelings and their friends. Protect them, provide for them, and then release them to bring your values into the next generation.

Melanie and I have six children, five boys and a girl. The five oldest are married and involved in our ministry with their spouses. My youngest is studying for ministry at a Bible college and developing a strong character and prayer life. We have had ups and downs through the years with their character and development, but thank God they are all serving the Lord!

I still recall the day our governor invited our entire family to a state luncheon in our honor. All six of them, ages six to twenty, sat quietly and politely eating and interacting with his staff in the state dining room. I thought to myself, *Melanie sure did a good job with these kids!* I am a proud papa, but I do realize that Melanie and I needed help. We couldn't do anything outside of God's power and grace. It's He who enabled us to be godly parents.

God wants *you* to have a model family. We have all made mistakes, but God can put your family back into divine order. God sees your inward *integrity* and *purity*, but it is the community who sees your outward *example*, portrayed best by a happy marriage and godly children.

———◦———

Integrity. Purity. Example. This is your character, the path to long-term *influence*.

If you have made it this far, you are ready to take the second step in becoming a model man: consistency, the path to long-term *success*.

DISCUSSION QUESTIONS

1. Think about your circle of influence. Who are the people in your life that God is calling you to be an example to?

2. Controlling your tongue and your emotions is never easy, particularly under pressure. What is the one situation you face in life that always seems to be the most difficult to control yourself in?

3. In a world full of rebellion, keeping the rules all the time is difficult. What is the rule that challenges you the most?

4. Order is from God. If the group were to do an inspection of your yard, closets, garage, auto, and workplace, what would they immediately see about you? Which area are you going to put in order first?

5. A model family is one where the husband assumes his responsibility as leader of his wife and children. Would you say that there is an area within your family dynamic that is out of order?

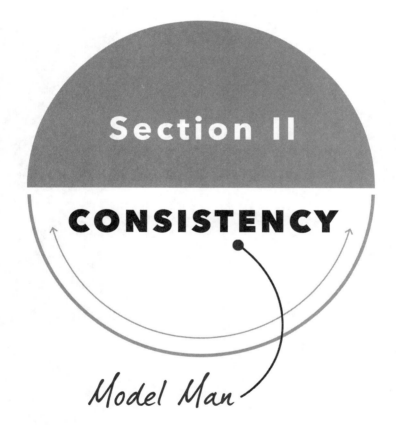

Section II

CONSISTENCY

Model Man

THE PACE OF GRACE

Let us lay aside every weight, and the sin
which so easily ensnares us, and let us run
*with **endurance** the race that is set before us.*
—HEBREWS 12:1, NKJV, emphasis added

OUTSIDE OF THE Louisiana State Capitol stands a thirty-five-foot bronze statue of former governor Huey P. Long. It looks exactly like him right down to his infamous smirk and persuasive eyes. The statue has stood fixed and immovable since its erection in 1940. Except for a few nicks and scrapes, it has never changed, even after enduring thirty-two hurricanes! Down through the years, gale-force winds have pounded it. Slashing rain and hail have beat on it. Birds have messed on it, and kids have climbed it! Yet consistently, year after year, when the storms have passed, old Huey is still standing there tall and steady. He's become a dependable fixture overlooking the Capitol grounds.

As a *model man,* your character should be like that statue—a fixed object that looks like you, perfectly symbolizes you, and stands immovable in the midst of the culture's relentless onslaughts. When the storms of the world rage all around, pounding you, your family, your marriage, and your workplace, those in your circle of influence are watching and wondering if your character is going to collapse. Some may be betting on your collapse. Yet after the winds and rains die down and they are sifting through the debris, there you'll be, standing strong and steady. As time passes and the storms of life come and go and you *consistently* stand, the people in your circle *will* begin to run to you for refuge.

Fixed

Immovable

Consistent

The character of the *model man* has *consistently* stood the test of time. He's weathered the storms and has now become a place of refuge for others. He can be counted on. That is the importance of your long-term *consistency*: people can predict that you will pass through the storms, the changes, and the whims of culture with *fixed* and *immovable* character.

Once your character is fixed and immovable, the next critical element in the development of *consistent* character is the understanding that you are running a race.

There *is* a goal.

There *is* a finish line.

And there *are* things that would hinder you from running well.

As a *model man*, you must be willing to drop the weights and sins in your life that are encumbering your progress. Could you imagine an Olympic athlete running for the gold in blue jeans and boots while holding twenty-pound dumbbells in each hand? Of course not! That would be crazy. To compete effectively, serious runners shed themselves of anything that would weigh them down and wear the lightest, most wind-resistant running gear possible. This should be your attitude towards the Christian life. Anything that is hindering your race has got to go!

To run effectively, you must also realize that the race you're running is a marathon, not a sprint. Understanding the difference is crucial. The Christian life is a race of *endurance*. It's about going the distance and finishing strong in life. Many men start the Christian race, shooting out of the blocks like they're running a forty-yard dash and are going to set the world on fire, but soon they are burned out and drop out. After being in the ministry for over thirty years, it saddens me to have seen so many men that started strong burn out and then drop out of the race. That's because they didn't understand the principle of *pace.*

IT'S ALL ABOUT PACE

The secret of running a marathon and finishing strong is pace. When watching distance races in the Olympics, it is amazing how one runner will inevitably jump out front and lead the entire pack for much of the race. Often the commentator reminds the audience, "Don't worry about him. He is running faster than a world-record pace." Then at some point close to the end of the race, the gold medalist starts his kick and easily surpasses the front-runner, who usually drops to the back of the pack from his overexertion. The seasoned champion runner has run his race with self-control, discernment, and timing. He's learned to *pace* himself. The *model man* must do the same if he is going to maximize his effectiveness in life and finish strong.

Many men today are living lives controlled by adrenaline. They are operating on energy and adrenaline rather than purpose and pace. Their lives, their marriages, and their relationships are imploding because of their exhausting pace. They are risking a meltdown, a brownout, acting like a short-term firecracker rather than a strategic long-range torpedo. Adrenaline is the fight-or-flight hormone in your body that gives you almost superhuman energy in a short burst to run from gunfire or remove a heavy object from someone trapped underneath. It achieves great results, but the problem is it cannot be sustained, and running on adrenaline causes undue stress. *The Scandinavian Journal of Public Health* reported in their study that stress actually has the ability to raise the cholesterol level in some individuals.[1]

Model men must learn the *pace of grace.*

MOSES AND THE PACE OF GRACE

As described in Exodus 18, Moses had come to a place in his life where his pace was about to kill him. By the power of God, he had struck Egypt with ten plagues, led perhaps two million people out of Egypt, crossed the Red Sea, killed Pharaoh's army, and defeated the Amalekites. You could say he'd had a pretty good season at 10-0!

His father-in-law, Jethro, came to Mount Sinai out in the desert, bringing Moses' wife and two boys with him.[2] Jethro hung around a few days, watching the hordes of people lining up all day around Moses' tent, waiting for him to render a verdict in their cases and lawsuits. Then Jethro spoke frankly with his son-in-law: *"What you are doing is not good. You and the people with you will certainly wear yourselves out, for the thing is too heavy for you"* (Exodus 18:17-18).

Thank God for someone who could confront Moses about his schedule! It took Jethro less than twenty-four hours to see how ridiculous Moses' lifestyle and *pace* had become. Sometimes we are so caught up in our responsibilities that we cannot see the long-term effect they will have both on us and on those who are depending on us.

Jethro gave Moses some life-changing advice on how to delegate to those who could make low-level "triage" decisions while he took the role of a "surgeon." This one little change would totally transform Moses' lifestyle and help him last the entire forty years that he would lead Israel through the desert: *"If you do this,"* Jethro said to him, *"God will direct you, you will be able to **endure**, and all this people also will go to their place in peace"* (Exodus 18:23, emphasis added).

Are you willing to make some decisions and modifications that will give you long-term success? I am going to list four things for you to focus on to step into the pace of grace.

1. Your Yoke

Jesus once declared, *"Come to me, all who labor and are heavy laden, and I will give you rest. Take my yoke upon you, and learn from me, for I am gentle and lowly in heart, and you will find rest for your souls. For my yoke is easy, and my burden is light"* (Matthew 11:28-30). Jesus is telling us that our first problem in getting outside the pace of grace is our yoke. We have assumed a burden that God did not intend for us to carry.

When you are training a young ox, you put him in the yoke with a seasoned ox who knows the *pace* to plow for an entire day. Of course, the young ox is gung ho and tries to pull ahead, but he cannot move the older ox outside his pace. Eventually he will lag behind and feel the same pinch again. In a short while, he discovers two things:

1. The old ox is really the one pulling the yoke. He is just walking beside him!

2. It is worthless, tiring, and frustrating to try to pull the old ox to go faster, because his pace is set.

This reminds me of my walk with Jesus.

First, the yoke is *His* yoke (*"Take my yoke upon you"*). He is the big ox; I am the learner. Paul said that we are *"working together with him"* (2 Corinthians 6:1).

Years ago, my father learned this secret as a denominational pastor. Someone asked him one time how he had learned to walk in the power of the Spirit. He replied, "I used to work *for* God. Now I work *with* God!"

Second, the yoke is my ego. Jesus continued, *"I am gentle and lowly in heart, and you will find rest for your souls"* (Matthew 11:29). There is the heart of the matter!

When you are meek and humble, you are not striving to be noticed and applauded. Many men who operate on an adrenaline flow have their eyes on the success of others with a bigger business, more successful ministry, or more properties and possessions.

Drive is a good thing. Without it, you will never succeed. But to be *driven* is a totally different issue. I don't believe in laziness or chilling out until success comes your way. In the same way, however, I don't believe in burning out so that my success is short-term and not long-term.

One of my father's best friends in ministry was Pastor John Osteen of Lakewood Church in Houston (Joel Osteen's father). He had built a large evangelistic organization with many employees. He was spending all his time traveling to raise money for the huge payroll he was carrying.

One day as he was praying, he saw in his mind a huge cross lying on the ground. A voice said to him, "Take up your cross and follow Me." He bent down to pick up this massive cross—and it flew up over his head like a feather. It was made out of Styrofoam! Immediately the verse came to him: *"My yoke is easy, and my burden is light."* In other words, God had not given him this huge staff; he had given it to himself! He scaled back to a skeleton staff and immediately returned to the pace of grace.

If the yoke and burden God gave you is easy and light, where did this thing you are carrying come from? Now you are analyzing your motives and your insecurities that are driving you forward.

Years ago, my major professor in college was in Israel. He looked out the window and noticed a shepherd walking behind a flock of sheep. He asked the guide, "Why is the shepherd walking behind the sheep instead of in front of the sheep?"

The guide laughed and responded, "That's not a shepherd. That's a butcher."

Satan *drives*, but Jesus *leads*.

I have watched pastors, business leaders, and a host of others in various occupations fall from a lofty position of leadership. They are so driven that they cannot see their family, their marriage, or the host of victims they have slain in their path to the top.

The opposite of that is Jesus, who promised *"rest for your souls."* The tired emotions of men who have fought until the sword froze to their hand (see 2 Samuel 23:10) have placed them upon the scrap heap of long-term success.

Jesus said, *"My Father is always at his work to this very day, and I too, am working"* (John 5:17, NIV). But that is not drivenness.

In college, I learned a great definition of the word *abide* in John 15: "working to full capacity in a relaxed state of faith." God expects us to work hard, to not have laziness anywhere around our character. However, He also expects us to inwardly remain relaxed, turning over the pressures and stress of success as we abide in Him.

2. Your Inner Circles

The pace of grace is about prioritizing the relationships in your life.

Many highly successful business and professional leaders are great networkers. They can work a room and stay in close contact with hundreds of people monthly. They try to please, prioritize, and prop up everyone in their lives. They don't appraise every relationship in terms of the time commitment it will cost. They spend time with those who demand time, rather than with those who deserve time.

In contrast, Jesus gave most of His time to the people closest to Him. He actually had concentric circles of relations, like a bull's-eye. First was His innermost circle of three disciples: Peter, James, and John. Then came the full group of twelve disciples. After that came the seventy

He sent out to do ministry. He poured the majority of His time and energy into preparing these powerful leaders who would change the world.

If you set up your life as a bull's-eye, who would be at the center of the target?

For me, it is my wife. I cannot imagine doing life and ministry without her. In fact, I have told her already, "If you leave me, I am going with you!"

Because she is the absolute center of my inner circle, I stay in touch with her hourly, or as close to it as possible. Whether I am at home or overseas, at least twice a day I get in contact with Melanie by phone, by text, or by FaceTime. When I am home, we text throughout the day, checking in with each other.

The second part of my inner circle is my family. I have six beautiful children, and I like to stay in touch with them daily, or close to it. They are scattered across the United States, but at least every couple of days they hear from me by phone or text.

They are my number-one disciples! I have spent more of my time with them than with any other people on earth. The older we all get, the closer we all get, and it is my joy to watch them exceed my success. In fact, my second son is now *my* pastor as I extend outside of the local church to reach pastors and men worldwide.

The outer ring of my bull's-eye is my spiritual sons. Throughout the years, I have accumulated a large group of spiritual leaders who look to me to father and mentor them. They are former staff members or pastors or captains in the movements I help to shepherd worldwide (Remnant pastors and Surge church planters). I try to stay in contact with this vital group weekly or monthly through a series of conference calls, mentoring lessons, or private contact I have with them.

Of course, I have other relationships too. But all these other realms (boards, committees, commissions, cabinets, and so on) are outside my closest rings of relationship, and I may serve them only periodically or annually. I have analyzed every group I am a part of in terms of the purposes God has called me to and not the influence it affords me. I am on only a couple of boards, and they are both highly strategic in terms of the advancement of the kingdom of God.

Now you are getting the picture. Who is your inner circle? Who has demonstrated by their faithfulness that they deserve quality, personal time with you? Who can you realistically feed, lead, and direct? Who has responded positively to input and even correction? Who has yielded fruit? Once you become totally focused on that inner circle, you will stop trying to *be* the Messiah and just simply *emulate* the Messiah.

3. Your Money

The third area of the pace of grace has to do with the huge pressure that money puts on your pace. Financial pressure eats away at you, stresses you out in the night, and never leaves your mind. Surely God did not intend for us to be living lives of anxiety and worry about things that ultimately equate to passing like a pilgrim through this world!

There is one word that will immediately take that pressure off you: *margins.*

While I am typing this page, my word processor automatically wraps the word of a sentence at the end of a line before the letters go over the margins of the page. I don't really like it sometimes, because I think I could fit more on a line! However, the margin allows me to type without looking at the page. Similarly, margins in our lives help us manage the accumulating demands on our finances.

Money is about margins. You have to set certain guidelines for yourself that keep you from amping up the pace of life just to barely make it financially.

- *Follow the 10/10/80 rule.* I always tithe 10 percent, save 10 percent, and live off 80 percent.

- *Establish a 90 percent budget.* Set your spending at 90 percent of your previous year's income. That way, if your income drops a little, you have a cushion built in to absorb it. If your income increases, you have money to apply to debt or to save.

- *Live off the top of the barrel.* Many people scrape the bottom of the barrel every time they have a need. They live from paycheck to paycheck, with no cash on hand for emergencies or opportunities. But a wise pastor taught me once that if you will "fill your barrel" once in your life, you can simply dip into the top of it when you have a need. In other words, you create an emergency fund. If you ever have to use any of those funds, you immediately turn your faith loose to replenish that "barrel."

- *Live below your means.* Usually, an extravagant lifestyle comes from inward insecurity. It is proving to yourself and everyone else that you have arrived. Cars and clothes keep most people in deep debt. They are embarrassed at the thought of driving a used car!

One man jokingly told my father, as they drove along in his new car, "Roy, you need to get delivered from that used-car demon."

Daddy replied, "I know; you're right. By the way, how much do you want for this one?" He could have afforded to buy it, but he didn't feel a need to.

We have all observed the wasteful, extravagant lifestyle of athletes and movie stars whose millions turned into pennies. But that's not the only way to live. Having visited the Walmart empire in Bentonville, Arkansas, I can tell you that one of their highest values is "living below your means." They have one of the largest corporations in America because they maintain their roots of value and frugality.

4. Your Opportunities

The last area of the pace of grace has to do with the things in life that look like they were sent from God to help you, when in fact they were sent from hell to distract you.

Opportunities are sudden, unexpected doorways apparently leading to future advancement. Usually, people are awed and flattered by opportunities. And in fact, some opportunities are clearly the hand of the Lord giving you a new job, a new house, or a new position. As a pastor, however, I have watched many of those great "opportunities" take a leader down, even when his intentions were wonderful.

Consider a biblical example: Joshua and the Gibeonites.

Joshua was on a roll. He had crossed the Jordan River, conquered Jericho and Ai, and had huge momentum going into the conquest of Canaan. Then, out of nowhere, came a group of men who said they had taken a long journey to get there. Their clothes, their footwear, their storage sacks all appeared to be dusty and moldy. They were disguised as foreigners, when in actuality they were Gibeonites, living right in Canaan. Their story appeared so legitimate that Joshua *"did not ask counsel from the LORD"* (Joshua 9:14) and made a treaty with them.

Within hours, their ruse was exposed, but the long-term damage in Israel's history was cemented. This was an "opportunity" that was really a sidetrack.

Satan is a master at giving us revolving doors that look like open doors. Revolving doors, if you get stuck in them, require great effort to go nowhere. One of Dad's friends went to New Orleans, bought an ice cream cone, and walked into his first revolving door. He said that he ate the whole cone of ice cream before he got out of it!

It is easy to jump at every opportunity: new properties, more locations, board positions, media opportunities, and so on. The question is, did God provide this opportunity, or has Satan sent it to sap your resources, personnel, and energy? Will it help you to accomplish what God has called you to do, or will it be a drain on the limited focus you presently have?

Years ago, we bought a media property that seemed to have the potential to open our entire city to the gospel.

We had visions of thousands of people getting right with the Lord. The opportunity was so amazing that we never really prayed a lot about it. After all, how could an opportunity like this not result in amazing growth and conversions? After five years, however, we had spent hundreds of thousands of dollars in operation and *could not find one person in our church who had received Christ as a result of that media outlet!*

Timing is critical in opportunities. God may be telling you to do something—but not at this moment. Jesus' brothers tried to push Him to go down to Jerusalem so that His fame and popularity could skyrocket (see John 7:3). *"My time has not yet come, but your time is always here"* was His response (verse 6).

An automobile burns the least fuel with the most power when the timing is set correctly. Relax in the pace of grace, trusting that the God who provided the opportunity will confirm the move with His financial provision.

———◆———

These four things—yoke, inner circles, margins, and opportunities—determine the *pace of grace.* It may be time for you to come aside for a while and reexamine your pace.

Let's look at a fifth and most important element of the pace of grace: discipline.

DISCUSSION QUESTIONS

1. In our high-pressure world, do you sometimes feel that the yoke you are carrying comes from your drivenness more than from Christ's direction?
2. Whom do you define as your inner circles? How often are you in touch with those within the circles?
3. Handling money effectively is about margins. What margins have you set for yourself that keep you from completely running out of money?
4. Everyone gets opportunities. What process do you use to help you get the mind of the Lord on whether an opportunity came from Him or the enemy?

NOTES

1. Anna Hodgekiss, "A stressful job really CAN kill you—by raising your cholesterol," Daily Mail, May 17, 2013, http://www.dailymail.co.uk/health/article-2326132/A-stressful-job-really-CAN-kill--raising-cholesterol.html.
2. We don't know why Moses' wife was not already with him, but in any case, it is important to remember that he was an outward success but a family failure.

POWER OVER YOURSELF

*If anyone desires to come after Me,
let him deny himself, and take up
his cross **daily**, and follow Me.*
—LUKE 9:23, NKJV, emphasis added

SO FAR WE'VE seen the significance of moving in the pace of grace in regards to developing *consistency* of character—walking with correct motives (yoke), focusing on the right people (inner circles), maintaining margins (money), and carefully discerning opportunities.

The fifth critical component of the pace of grace is an area all its own: discipline. Pace is all about discipline. It is the tortoise-and-hare approach to life, doing the right things *consistently* and daily. Others may be zooming ahead, laughing at your plodding, ordered tempo. Let's look, however, at the end of the story.

Jesus said, *"If anyone would come after me, let him deny himself and take up his cross **daily** and follow me"* (Luke 9:23, emphasis added). Somewhere down the line, your daily schedule of life must undergo a makeover. You are who you are because of the *daily* schedule you have maintained.

True pace is when your godly, attainable schedule is implemented with a consistent routine of accomplishment. *That* is discipline.

Notice that I referred to your *attainable* schedule. Have you ever been to the doctor's office and waited in three different waiting rooms? Each place has magazines, so they know you will be waiting in that room also, even if you feel like you are moving up in line. Do you know why that is? Doctors try to cram in too many patients in a day, assuming there will be some no-shows.

If you assume too much responsibility, you'll be stressed and frantic, throwing the schedule of your life out of balance because it will be impossible to sustain. I chuckled once when the governor told me, "You are the busiest man I know." He was right—I do keep very busy. But I'm not frantic. There is a difference between what is important and what is attainable.

Years ago Charles Hummel wrote a powerful little book titled *Tyranny of the Urgent.* In it, he points out how we too often get caught in the trap of letting the urgent things in life take rule over the important things. When we do, life becomes a frantic chase to put out fires rather than a steady rhythm of harmony. The really important things get left undone, and the really important relationships get cheated. But you do have a choice. You can say no to the urgent and yes to the important. It takes *discipline*. Below are some disciplines I try to incorporate into my schedule to make sure I'm staying in the pace of grace. I believe they will help you too.

YOUR DEVOTIONAL SCHEDULE (DAILY)

Jesus was a very busy person, with people demanding His attention every day, yet He never neglected His relationship with His Father. On the contrary, He prioritized it. For example, one day, *"rising very early in the morning, while it was still dark, he departed and went out to a desolate place, and there he prayed"* (Mark 1:35). Somehow, despite his demanding schedule, Jesus managed to maintain the pace of grace. His days started with prayer and often ended in prayer. His whole life was a journey from one place of prayer to the next, with activity in between. Yet we all think we are too busy to pray! Martin Luther once said, "I have so much to do that I shall spend the first three hours in prayer." I'm not saying you have to spend three hours a day in prayer like Luther, but it's amazing how we justify being too busy to pray. Are we busier than Jesus Himself? The truth is we are too busy *not* to pray!

Always start every day with the Word of God and prayer. Prayer does not *waste* your time; it *saves* you time!

I heard about a couple of guys who were chopping wood in an eight-hour contest. One of them never stopped working, but the other would often go sit under a tree for a few minutes. At the end of the day, to the nonstop chopper's surprise, the one who had repeatedly stopped his work had cut more wood than he. The loser asked the winner how he did it, to which he replied, "When I stopped, I was sharpening my ax."

I learned years ago that if I take time to pray and read the Word of God every morning, I can make eight decisions in an hour. However, if I don't take time to pray, it can take me eight hours to make one decision!

For my book *The Remnant,* I wrote a whole chapter on the prayer life, particularly on the subject of tabernacle prayer. Over twenty years ago, I learned about the powerful method of praying through the various objects God put into the tabernacle. It's a wonderful way of approaching God devotionally.

There are many good daily templates to help guide your prayer time. Some people like to meander as they pray, praying *however* and *whatever* comes to their minds.

My problem with that is that too much comes to my mind, especially things I am supposed to be doing that day! So instead I prefer to follow a track, whether it is topically praying the Lord's Prayer, praying through a Bible passage, or starting with the blessings of the cross (the brazen altar) and ending with the throne of God (the ark) in the tabernacle. The primary thing is to really contact God, sensing His presence and fellowship in a real and vital way.

This is how you have to start your day! It may not be still dark, as it was when Jesus prayed, but it has to be early enough that you have a relaxed time of fellowship with the Lord before entering the *hurricane* of your daily life.

I also have a systematic Bible reading plan. In 1990, President Bush decreed that year as the Year of the Bible and encouraged all Americans to read through the Bible in one year. I introduced our church to the *One Year Bible* plan, a fifteen-minute-a-day plan to complete the whole Bible in one year. Thousands participated as I taught on Sundays from the Old Testament readings that week and on Wednesdays from the New Testament readings. (I eventually wrote a devotional for it called the *One Year Devotional*.)

We're still doing it! Almost twenty-five years later, thousands would not start their day without it. This is a simple, attainable part of your daily schedule that will produce amazing results in your life, your business, and your family.

YOUR WORK SCHEDULE (WEEKLY)

A second important discipline for your schedule is how much you work every week. Try not to work over fifty hours a week. (That's six days of about eight hours a day or five days of ten hours a day.) When I say "work," I am referring to time away from your family. That means that Little League coaching and volunteering need to be included in that amount. In essence, it's the *responsibilities* that take you outside the home.

I know that many people are working sixty to eighty hours weekly to "make ends meet" or to "get ahead." If that includes you, then please realize that in terms of your family and your health, *you are not really getting ahead.* You cannot sustain that pace! Readjust your lifestyle to fit within the income you can physically provide in a realistic schedule.

I read about one lady in China who was working 128 hours a week. You can do that and live half a life if you want to! Forty to fifty hours a week should be sufficient for you to complete your tasks and still have time for a Sabbath day of total rest and refreshing.

The Sabbath principle is critical for long-term success. If God took one, why shouldn't you? The Sabbath is not only a day for worship in God's house, but also a total break from work so that you can spend time with your family and those you love the most. I recommend that you schedule two days off a week, because inevitably you will get into something unexpected with work, home, or responsibilities and one of those days will disappear. I've dealt with men for a long time, so I know this might be one of the most important reading moments for you in this book.

This is where the rubber meets the road.

Your Planning Schedule (Monthly)

Try to do a two- or three-day fast or retreat every month.

For years, I have set the focus of a month on the first three days for planning every day, preparing myself for every day, and then praying through the entire month. Often I have fasted from solid foods and just had liquids and juices.

You'd be amazed at how clear your mind becomes on the third day of a juice fast! Decisions that you have been unable to make suddenly become obvious. Esther did a three-day fast. Ezra did a three-day fast. Something breaks open in your life when you focus on the Lord during a three-day period.

Select three good days for you at the beginning of a month. Fast one meal a day or, if you are able, three full days. You are disciplining yourself to seek the Lord for His guidance and direction with your business, your finances, your children, and your decisions. I've done this for so many years that I hardly notice I am fasting until the third day—and that's when things really start to shift!

By the way, I don't have to be led to fast. Jesus said, *"When you fast . . ."* like *"When you pray . . ."* (Matthew 6:5,16). No one even needs to hardly notice that you are missing a meal or two. In your heart, however, you know that you are deeply pursuing God for His wisdom and direction in your life. What an awesome discipline to put into your schedule!

Your Yearly Schedule

I like the feeling when an odometer turns over to nothing but zeros. January 1 feels like that to me. It's time for change, time for renewal, time for a new me!

For many years, I have taken the first part of January (up to twenty-one days) for an extended time to do what I do monthly: focused pursuit of God through Bible reading, prayer, and fasting. I have even done a Daniel fast several times, eating only fruits, vegetables, and water (see Daniel 1:12). Thousands have joined me in this pursuit and have had amazing breakthroughs in their health, their finances, and spiritual warfare.

Daniel experienced this in a twenty-one-day period of prayer: *"In those days, I, Daniel, was mourning for three weeks. I ate no delicacies, no meat or wine entered my mouth, nor did I anoint myself, for the full three full weeks"* (Daniel 10:2-3). At the end of those days, an angel touched him and said that he had been dispatched from heaven on the very first day of Daniel's three weeks but had been resisted by a *"prince of the kingdom of Persia"* (Daniel 10:13) for three weeks.

I was in one of these January seasons when I passed the governor's mansion located in Baton Rouge. Suddenly, in my Spirit, I saw a wind blow open the door of the mansion. I told my wife, "I believe God is going to open a door to the governor's mansion for a Bible study this year." Within one week, his office called mine saying that the governor had been on his treadmill, had seen my ninety-second TV program, and wanted me to teach him the whole Bible in four lessons! I ended up going every Wednesday for six years to teach the Bible to him and his top staff.

I challenge you to try it next January and see if this focus in your schedule does not make an amazing difference in the entire twelve months of the year.

YOUR FAMILY SCHEDULE

In a fast-paced world, believe me, it takes *discipline* to not allow your family to be shoved to the backseat of life only to get the leftovers from business and pleasure. When my family was young, I made a choice to implement three specific disciplines into my schedule. Eventually I would look back on that choice as one of the most important decisions of my life.

1. Weekly family night (more about this in chapter 8). My wife's father taught me how to do this, and I saw the results it had in my wife's life. Every Monday night (since Monday was my day off), we had family night. We wrestled on the floor, popped popcorn, played "Wolf" in the house, watched movies, and just had a blast for several hours. No one and nothing could interrupt this most important time of the week for our family, and my children still talk about it as one of the greatest memories of their childhood.

2. Weekly date night. You may have been married thirty-seven years like me, but you still need to romance your wife! She deserves a little get-out-of-the-house time with you, even if you don't have any money and just walk around downtown or on a trail. It may require a babysitter, but it's an investment in the most important person and relationship you have. You will be amazed at how you reconnect weekly as she anticipates that little time set aside specially just for her.

Don't bring a friend, don't bring the kids, and don't make her cook! The more thought you put into it, the more special it will be to her. Keep the conversation positive, intellectual, and intimate, not just wolfing down a hamburger and then heading home.

3. Yearly family vacation. I know guys who tell me that they are too busy or that it is too expensive to take a vacation. Really? Can you replace time in the woods, time at the beach, time at a theme park, time on a houseboat, time in the mountains?

Our memories as a family generally center on the pristine conditions we found as we camped all over America. We tubed down creeks, slid down water cascades, fished in canyons, rode rides, roasted wieners, dove for sand dollars, and had many other memorable moments together.

Inevitably, something would come up the day before we left on a well-planned trip together that would raise a question of whether we could even go. Early on, I made a decision: "It will all be there when I get back. It will not all fall into a hole. But if it does, just prepare to start over after the family vacation!"

Find a state park and rent one of their cabins by the lake for a week. Buy a tent and Coleman stove and rough it. When you have more money, take in a water park and theme park or travel through states with gorgeous scenery. Your relationship with your children is going to be based, not upon how *much* you provided, but how *well* you provided a lifetime full of fun, bonding, and meaning.

YOUR HEALTH SCHEDULE

Now we come to the last discipline in your schedule that will keep you in the pace of grace: the discipline of your physical life (sleep, exercise, and eating). You would be surprised at how important these are to a *consistent* life of success. I'm no fitness or dietary expert, but I will tell you what I have done to strengthen these areas in my own life.

1. Go to bed and get up in a timely way. The earlier you go to sleep, the better your sleep. Many guys are up late, hours after their wife goes to bed. They ramble around the kitchen and TV room, fixing late-night snacks and watching late-night television, often allowing sinful images and ideas to enter their minds. Not only do they drift further and further apart from their wife emotionally, but also their sexual life suffers and their daily schedules become opposite. If possible, try to go to bed together and wake up together. Take a hot bath between 9:30 and 10:00 and then hit the sack, ready to get up early for prayer, exercise, and fellowship together.

2. Have a daily exercise routine. Most mornings, Melanie and I start our day with a two-mile walk. It is right by our home on a little course that we can mindlessly power walk without keeping up with watches, timers, and distance meters. If you are a serious fitness guy, you would probably laugh at what I do. However, I don't see many others out walking in the mornings (rain, cold, or shine), so I figure I am ahead of the game!

I've also read that you lose about 2 percent of your muscle mass every year over fifty, so I also try to lift weights three days a week. I know I will never be Arnold Schwarzenegger, but I am interested primarily in stretching and toning. For a while (before I invested in some dumbbells), I went to a gym close by. In going to the gym those three times a week, I discovered what the most difficult machine is in the health club—the front door!

Everyone *talks* about working out, but not many *do* it. You can find sideline fitness gurus everywhere, but when you ask them what they are doing, they say, "Soon I am going to begin to proceed to commence to start!"

Find something you can do consistently. Get a partner who will work out with you. Remember to do something lest you do nothing. Don't listen to those who say you are not doing enough. It reminds me of my dad, who used to lie in bed and count my mother's sit-ups every morning.

If she didn't touch her elbows to her knees, he would say, "Wait a minute. That one didn't count!"

3. Eat earlier in the day. My wife stays slender, and I asked her about her diet. From her I learned this principle: Eat like a *king* for breakfast (your biggest meal of the day), like a *prince* for lunch (salad and sandwich), and like a *pauper* for supper (something light and nothing after 7:00 p.m.). I have tried it over the last few years and have lost about fifteen pounds that have stayed off.

I told one of the overweight guys on staff about Melanie's diet, and he tried it. Later, I asked him how it was coming, and he said, "Great! I eat like a king for breakfast, like a prince for lunch, and like a pauper for supper. The only thing is that about 10:30 at night I hear a little voice within me that says, 'Long live the king!'"

We laugh a lot about food in our home because we love to eat. Who doesn't? Melanie cooks wonderful, healthy meals for our family—nothing fried, primarily chicken, whole wheat everything, plenty of veggies, salads, soups and gumbos, beans of all varieties. You get the picture. You can alter your whole life by learning to discipline yourself away from sweets, fast food, fatty meats, starches, and heavy cheeses.

Don't go on a drastic weight-loss plan. Simply discipline yourself to eat at regular times with reasonable portions of good food. Weight will slowly drop off you until you get down to a sustainable weight for life. Your high-intensity, cram-it-on-the-go, road-warrior lifestyle is adding ten pounds a year to your already overburdened knees. One guy told me that he had to eat all day to stay as big as he is! Cut out the grazing every hour in the pantry and refrigerator, and discipline yourself to eat at mealtimes.

Bam! There it is—lifestyle makeover. Stepping into a schedule that is attainable and disciplined. In the Word, close to God, close to your wife and kids, sleeping right, exercising, and eating right. Not just for this month, but for life. Do these things five years and see what type of person you look at in the mirror. None of them costs you any more money, just time in your schedule and regular, sustainable habits.

I have one further thought on *consistency* before we deal with your relationships. It has to do with the one force in life that moves you forward through storms, trials, disappointments, loss, adversity, confusion, and change:

Purpose.

DISCUSSION QUESTIONS

1. Discuss your daily devotional life in Bible reading and prayer. What has worked for you?

2. Balancing work and family is a challenge. Work always seems to take priority. What limits do you have on yourself about how much you work?

3. Talk about a weekly family night and date night. What changes do you need to make to be sure your inner circles are getting the time they need with you?

4. Health is based on eating, sleeping, and exercise. Which area of those three is the biggest challenge for you?

CHAPTER

6

LIVING A LIFE
OF PURPOSE

If only I may finish my course....
—ACTS 20:24, emphasis added

YEARS AGO, I heard a story of a psychologist who was studying productivity. He hired men at eight dollars an hour to cut wood in his backyard while he observed their behavior from the house. The only requirement to be paid was that they had to cut the wood with the back side of the ax!

One fellow was banging away in the backyard, and the psychologist went away from the window for a minute to get something. When he returned, he heard a commotion in the backyard. The man was wildly cutting with the *edge* side of the ax.

The psychologist ran outside and said, "You are disqualifying yourself from getting paid. You are using the sharp side of the ax."

The man replied, "I don't care if I am getting paid or not—I've got to see some chips fly!"

Have you ever felt that way in your job, in your family, in your business? You feel yourself endlessly walking around the mill like a blinded Samson, full of power and potential but relegated to a loss of purpose. Everyone is caught up in activity. But activity without purpose becomes mindless, boring, and depressing.

Consistency is indeed about pace—pace of drive, pace of relationships, pace of finances, pace of opportunities, and pace of discipline. Yet there is one final area that ties all of them together. That area is *purpose*. Without *purpose*, none of it works.

OTHERS

I have found an overarching purpose that takes me through the mountains and valleys, the losses and gains, the thick and the thin—*others*.

William Booth, founder of the Salvation Army, was an invalid at eighty-one. He could not make the annual conference and was asked to send a telegram to the thousands of delegates gathered. He thought for days about a one-word message that would embody his entire life's work. When they opened the telegram at the conference, the moderator read simply one word on the page: "OTHERS."

Your life is here and will soon be gone. I'm sure you've heard it said that you are living "in the dash." Your life is the small dash between your birthday and your death day on your tombstone.

One man whose life profoundly affected me to live "in the dash" was one of the greatest missionaries in Mexico's history, Daniel Ost. Brother Danny, as he was known nationwide, had a huge radio audience and planted gigantic Faith, Hope, and Love Centers that seated up to five thousand in the cities of Mexico.

When Danny was buried, he had requested to be buried on a hillside in Mexico City where thousands of unmarked graves were the final resting place for the poorest of the poor. Every day an average of fifty bodies were laid in nameless graves in that burial ground.

Danny was buried there under a large white cross, under a huge gravestone engraved with the name of his church and telephone numbers to call. Inside the small fenced-in yard around his grave was a *rack full of gospel tracts kept stocked by the church members.* At any given point in the day, you could see a crowd of mourners gathered around Danny's grave, reading the gospel literature to be saved.

I have never known another man whose purpose was so defined that he made preparations to win people to Christ after his death as much as during his life!

JESUS' EXAMPLE OF PURPOSE

Christ's goal was not to *prolong* His life, but to fulfill the *purpose* for His life.

Isaiah prophesied about Jesus, saying, *"I have set my face like a flint, and I know that I shall not be put to shame"* (Isaiah 50:7). And that's just how Jesus was. *"When the days drew near for him to be taken up, he set his face to go to Jerusalem"* (Luke 9:51).

Purpose drives you forward toward your divine assignment.

We can see it in the example of Christ, who only days before His hideous crucifixion was marching like a soldier toward Jerusalem. Instead of being timid and fearful, dragging His feet toward His bloody end, He *walked ahead*: *"They were on the road, going up to Jerusalem, and Jesus was walking ahead of them. And they were amazed, and those who followed were afraid"* (Mark 10:32).

Paul was the same as he went toward his death in Rome. *"Imprisonment and afflictions await me,"* he said. *"But I do not count my life of any value nor as precious to myself, if only I may finish **my** course"* (Acts 20:23-24, emphasis added).

As a *model man*, you have a specific course, a lane, to run your race in.

Indeed, all of the leaders of the early church died with a purpose, starting with Stephen and ending with John, the author of Revelation. They lived and died for others, wanting just one more day in life in order to affect another person with the gospel of Jesus Christ.

I was amazed to read in a Delta flight magazine recently about a course at Harvard Business School for business leaders.[1] At a cost of $13,000, the executives study absolutely nothing about business. Instead, for six days they study four areas: character, purpose, integrity, and values. Wow! You can save a lot of money by reading this book!

The article described an activity that each executive starts the weeklong course with. Each person is asked to contemplate through the first night of the week this question: "If you were on your deathbed conversing with your granddaughter about what was important in life, what would you say?" They are told to bring their answer to a small group and discuss it the next morning as the basis for the week.

Have you ever thought about *your* priorities? What would you tell your granddaughter is of highest importance in life?

Purpose is about priorities. It is about finding your mission and remaining focused on it.

A Wi-Fi or cellular signal can easily drift in and out so that you are suddenly disconnected. You have to recall or reconnect to your party and platform. Similarly, without priorities and purpose, you may drift for days, months, or even years, wasting the precious moments God has given you on the earth.

To more effectively convey the priorities of life, I want to use an illustration of two trees:

1. The tree of influence building. Recently I've noticed that a huge priority for many in our world is to gain influence. Through social media, networking, conferences, travel, and any other means possible, the goal is to get noticed and become more and more recognized.

I call this *the tree of influence building.* I have even heard recently of people *buying* Twitter followers so that their Twitter account will appear more influential! Whatever it takes, by whatever means, they feel they have got to get themselves out there, climb the tree, outshine others to become more influential. Their money, their business, their status is not an end in itself, but a means to the end of more influence.

The interesting thing to me is to observe the lives of men who climb that tree. It seems that the higher they get toward the top, the smaller and more brittle the branches become. No wonder men reach the pinnacle of their profession only to find themselves plunging back to reality from a fall! What took them a lifetime to achieve may be over in a period of days or even hours.

The root of the tree of influence building is ambition. Ambition can be defined as *the insatiable drive to please and be celebrated by others.* The Greek word *erithea* is about a politician who manipulates his way into office. It describes a selfish, driven person who will stop at nothing to achieve his ends. His goals justify his means. His intense desire of achievement is to make himself look bigger. He is fiercely competitive, driven forward by a sense of insecurity and ego.

Ambition employs all the tactics of the world: persuasion, manipulation, deception, gossip, betrayal, and anger. Political battles are breeding grounds for selfish ambition. The ambitious see strife as their opportunity to move upward; others see strife as a deadly enemy that must be reconciled and ended.

2. The tree of pleasing God. The other tree you can climb in life is the one that Jesus, Paul, William Booth, Danny Ost, and a host of others invested their lives in pursuing: the tree of pleasing God.

Jesus said of the heavenly Father, *"He has not left me alone, for I always do the things that are pleasing to him"*

(John 8:29). From the very first day of Jesus' baptism, God said to Him, *"This is my beloved Son, with whom I am well pleased"* (Matthew 3:17). At the Mount of Transfiguration, He again heard God say, *"This is my beloved Son, with whom I am well pleased"* (Matthew 17:5).

What tree was Jesus climbing? His relaxed *consistency* came from knowing that His character, His purity, His consistency, and His daily purpose were all bringing God great pleasure.

Paul climbed that tree his entire life: *"We also have as our ambition …to be pleasing to Him"* (2 Corinthians 5:9, NASB). Paul woke up each morning, whether in jail, on a shipwrecked island, or in a governor's palace, with one desire: to be pleasing to God.

At the root of this beautiful tree is the root of serving others. The human heart has to be in rhythm. When a heart is out of rhythm, there are many physical symptoms (dizziness, shortness of breath, weakness, and fatigue)— all of which are bad! Heart patients can feel the moment their heart goes from irregular back to regular, just like a car changing gears.

Ambition and its fruit of influence building is an "irregular heartbeat." God made you as a servant of others, not as a driving, manipulative "tree climber" who lives to see his name lifted higher and higher above all other names. When you live each day for serving others, your inner man goes back into rhythm.

Jesus taught, *"When you do all the things which are commanded you, say, 'We are unworthy slaves; we have done only that which we ought to have done'"* (Luke 17:10, NASB). Serving is our lifestyle, our calling, our motivation. We live to give, live to serve, live to love. You may even feel your heart going back into rhythm just thinking and meditating on this high, lofty spiritual purpose to live out your days.

Serving your family, serving the lost and broken, serving the least and last is a purpose that will never change in this crazy world that can flip in an hour. Your wealth may evaporate, your job may disappear, your influence may wane, but you never stop getting up each day saying, "Lord, what can I do today to bring You pleasure? And whom may I serve today in Your name?"

THREE PARTS OF PURPOSE

I have written a second book I would like to refer you to, *The Surge*. It details my personal passion for planting churches around the world. Since 2000, the Surge Project has been able to plant over twenty-two thousand churches in twelve huge world zones where national leaders are trained and financed to start their own churches.

The three principles I use for my own personal purpose and mission will apply to yours as well:

1. Your mandate. A mandate is something you will die to achieve.

I visited Blenheim Palace in England, the home of Winston Churchill. As I walked through the halls and library of that magnificent home, the voice of Churchill was playing his most famous speeches over a speaker system throughout the house. I bought the tapes and listened to all his speeches for three months in my car.

What gripped me was Churchill's purpose. He knew that Britain was fighting for the future of Western civilization. Try this one on for size:

> Hitler knows that he will have to break us in this island or lose the war. If we can stand up to him, all Europe may be free and the life of the world may move forward into broad, sunlit uplands. But if we fall, then the whole world, including the United States, including all that we have known and cared for, will sink into the abyss of a new Dark Age made more sinister, and perhaps more protracted, by the lights of perverted science.
>
> Let us therefore *brace ourselves to our duties*, and so bear ourselves that, if the British Empire and

its Commonwealth lasts for a thousand years, men will still say, "This was their finest hour!"[2]

That's what I'm talking about: *mandate*. I'm told that Churchill was up until four in the mornings dictating letters to his secretary. His tireless, focused priority was to defend our civilization from a demonic madman who was at that moment murdering millions of Jewish people.

As I write this book for men worldwide, I feel a sense of divine mandate and urgency about our world. My purpose in life is not to lower my golf handicap (though I love golf), to catch a prize fish, to kill another deer, to rev another car engine, or to attend another game. My mandate is 7 billion people on the planet Earth, 5 billion of whom are without Christ.

I did a quick mathematical calculation and discovered that those 5 billion people would stretch in a single-file line all the way around the entire equator of the planet, not just once, but *thirty-seven times!* That's my mandate. I get up and go to bed every day asking myself, *What did I do today to serve, love, and reach those thirty-seven lines of humanity who wait for even one crumb of the bread of life?*

Get yourself a mandate: serving people and pleasing God. In whatever form your mandate focuses for you, get it clearly in your sights and go for it with all your might, your passion, your money, your time, your energy, and your influence. Get your heart back in rhythm and feel the freedom, peace, joy, fulfillment, and blessing in what Jesus said: *"It is more blessed to give than to receive"* (Acts 20:35).

The former bishop of Baton Rouge, a friend of mine, died of cancer. They laid his body on a slab in the cathedral in no casket with his vestments and shoes on. There's the end. People passed his body by the thousands to pay their respects to someone who lived to serve.

The wife of one of my assistant pastors was killed in an automobile accident on her way to church. Almost fifteen hundred people attended her funeral, a record for our church. Upon investigating, I discovered that she and her husband had taken in fourteen different teenagers at crisis moments in their lives (a divorce, a failure, a habit) and raised them as their own. She cooked for these kids every day and drove them all to their respective schools. Many became bankers and other respected professionals. They all brought their families, their little ones, and their employees to this massive funeral for one housewife who lived the divine mandate—others.

2. *Your method.* What has God called you particularly to in serving others and pleasing Him? Plan your work and work your plan.

People have developed many methods to serve others. Some reach out to children and kids. Some devote their gifts to training in job skills. Some lead a small group for young married couples. Some mentor a recovering addict. Some stock food-pantry shelves. Some help the homeless and the abused. Some assist the elderly, bringing them joy in life's closing days. Some fix up widows' homes and look after their needs. Think of the millions of needs our world struggles to meet every day, and *surely* there is a purpose for you.

One of our men, Roger, came out of a drug-abuse background. After meeting Christ, Roger led a weekly Bible study at O'Brien House, a halfway house in Baton Rouge. He taught the men, cared for them, and brought them weekly to services as he fulfilled his regular job doing an early-morning newspaper route.

Now Roger has been hired at our Lazarus Project as the primary mentor and coach for the twelve young men there who are struggling to recover. Teams of men counsel and mentor these young men who are now delivered from their habit, free from their legal issues, and moving forward in life.

Your mandate will dictate your method. Love *will* find a way.

3. Your money. Zacchaeus was a rich businessman, but he was very short (see Luke 19:1-10). You will remember that he climbed up in a tree. What a picture of a man who had everything, ruthlessly stepping on others to climb the tree of stature, power, and wealth! The only thing wrong with him was the emptiness he felt once he got up into that tree.

Jesus called him to come down and prepare a meal for Him. After supper, Zacchaeus rose and said, *"Behold, Lord, half of my possessions I will give to the poor, and if I have defrauded anyone of anything, I will give back four times as much"* (verse 8, NASB).

Wow! Zacchaeus changed from the tree of influence building to the tree of pleasing God! He was saved, and his heart now longed to climb the tree of serving others and pleasing God. He donated half of his net worth to the poor. He no longer tried to fulfill his purpose with trinkets and toys accumulated in some closet. The joy of his life became meeting the needs of others and serving the Lord with all of his heart.

I mention your finances last in the study of purpose because often it is the most tangible way you can serve others. You use your money either to build influence or to serve people. Jesus said, *"You cannot serve God and money"* (Luke 16:13). Accumulating more and more wealth is not a purpose in life, but a channel through which you can serve more and more people.

———————————————

Find your purpose—your mandate, method, and money. Live to serve. Climb the tree of pleasing God.

Focus on the priorities. I believe that when you are on your deathbed, with your granddaughter sitting beside you, you will be able to tell her what life is all about and what priorities are worth pursuing.

And it didn't even cost you $13,000.

DISCUSSION QUESTIONS

1. If your granddaughter were sitting on the side of your deathbed, what would you tell her needed to be her priorities in life?

2. The tree of ambition and influence building is what many men are climbing today. Discuss an example in your life of someone who climbed to the top of that tree only to suffer a terrible fall back to earth.

3. The tree of serving and pleasing God is what Jesus and Paul spent their lives climbing. Discuss how God delivered you from building influence and showed you your eternal purpose and satisfaction in pleasing Him.

4. Your mandate, method, and money go along with your passion and purpose. What would you say right now is the mandate on your life, and what are you doing to accomplish it?

NOTES

1. Eric Lucas, "The Enlightened Leader," Sky, September 2013, 106.

2. Winston Churchill, "This Was Their Finest Hour," (June 18, 1940, House of Commons, London, England), in Suzanne McIntire and William E. Burns, eds., *Speeches in World History* (New York: Infobase Publishing, 2009), 348, emphasis added.

Section III

CONNECTIONS

Model Man

MAKING MAMA HAPPY

Husbands, live with your wives
*in an **understanding** way.*
—1 PETER 3:7, emphasis added

THUS FAR IN this book, we have learned that a *model man's character* and *consistency* produce long-term impressions on those around him. It matters not if our circle of influence is large or small; we can change a nation by making positive impressions one person at a time. Now we have reached the third and final section of this book: *Connections.*

Connections are all about relationships.

Depending upon your choices in life, there are three long-term relationships where others will look to you as a model: being a model husband, a model parent, and a model mentor.

Men struggle with relationships in general, but they particularly struggle in the relationship with their wife. Stumbling around like blind dogs in a meat house, we know something good is in there, if we could only find it! We feel our way around in the dark, living with this person who has a totally different view of life and is wired with a totally different set of emotions than ours. There was a best-selling book out years ago titled *Men Are from Mars, Women Are from Venus*. It's true! Or so it seems.

No wonder Peter said, *"Husbands, live with your wives in an **understanding** way, showing honor to the woman as the weaker vessel, since they are heirs with you of the grace of life, so that your prayers will not be hindered"* (1 Peter 3:7, emphasis added). There are some things you have to *understand* about your wife.

The psalmist wrote about a man who understands and nurtures his wife: *"Your wife will be like a fruitful vine within your house"* (Psalm 128:3). It literally means "a flower in the center of your house." She is going to be so happily married to you that she will *flourish* right in the center of your home. Though you are the leader of your family, she controls the environment. In other words, *if Mama ain't happy, ain't nobody happy!*

The question is, how do we get Mama happy? What are the things that make for a happy, flourishing wife instead of a hurt, sour, defeated, miserable wife? Much of it has to do with your *understanding* of her.

Personally, I've made seven major mistakes over the thirty-seven years of my marriage to Melanie. I'm sure you've made none of them, but just in case I'm wrong about that, you'll understand what is causing *your* wife to be so unhappy. Try to implement into your own marriage these seven things I have corrected (and continue to correct) in mine. Watch and see if it doesn't totally transform your home.

1. FINANCIAL INSECURITY

For some reason, I did not know how important financial security was to a wife. I had no savings for years. Totally relaxed, I lived by faith that every month God would supply all our needs. Meanwhile, Melanie stayed continually nervous and worried about our financial security even though we had never been late on a bill. I had no understanding that since the fall of man, men and women have been programmed differently.

When God told Eve, *"Your desire shall be for your husband, and he shall rule over you"* (Genesis 3:16), He was programming a woman to feel a deep desire, a need, and a vulnerability for a man. Otherwise, why would she even want to hang around you?

A woman is attracted to your security. I know that you think she was attracted to your great looks and sculpted physique, but actually she felt a sense of security that you would take care of her and her children for life. No wonder some of the most beautiful women in the world are married to some of the ugliest men in the world!

When things go bump in the night, she turns over and nudges you to say that she just heard something in the house. Of course, you turn over and tell her, "Go check it out!" She clings to the covers until you drag yourself out of bed, stroll into the kitchen, and see that it was dishes shifting in the sink. When Barney Fife returns with the coast-is-clear sign, she sighs in relief and hugs you and tells you that you are her security.

This tells us something about finances. Usually, men don't feel insecurity about finances. They mail off the house payment and don't worry about it again for twenty-nine more days. The wife, however, is always worried about finances. She wants to know not only where *this* payment is coming from, but also where the payment *three months from now* is coming from. Your reply? "From the same place this house payment came from. We'll have it when we need it. Relax!"

The only problem is, she can't relax. She envisions being kicked out of her home, her kids jerked from private school, vienna sausages for supper, and clothes from the Salvation Army.

The solution? Three months of salary in the bank. That principle is espoused by financial guru Dave Ramsey as the very first principle of financial freedom. When Mama can look in the bank and see the money needed for three months away, she gets happy!

You say, "How am I going to get that money?"

You are going to have to turn on the big guns: sell anything and everything you are no longer using (including that old boat behind the garage). Liquidate any part of your net worth that is not cash and put it in your emergency fund.

It may take you a number of months to "fill your barrel" (as I put it in chapter 4), but once you get it filled, you will keep it filled. This emergency fund means that if an air-conditioner compressor goes out, the family is no longer in peril. You fix it—*bam!*—and go about refilling your emergency fund. Mama gets real happy.

Of course, you want to fix any area where she feels insecure. For one thing, you need life insurance. You don't *think* you're going to die someday; you *know* you're going to die! What will be that security for her and your children if you suddenly are gone? She also worries over catastrophic illness. So be sure you have some type of health policy that will hedge your family against a total-loss medical condition.

When she sees that you have become serious about providing long-term financial security for her and her children, she is going to grab you, hug you, and kiss your face off!

First problem solved.

2. LONELINESS

The second issue I did not understand about a wife was her need for continual, deep, intimate fellowship with her man. Many wives are lonely!

You may say, "I know my wife is not lonely. I'm there every day after work until bedtime."

Really? What you really do is head straight to the couch, pick up a remote control with five hundred channels, open the newspaper, open your laptop to surf the Internet, and put your smartphone on the couch arm so that you can monitor your incoming e-mails, texts, and Twitters.

I've been told we all need to speak about 25,000 words a day. Perhaps you are gone all day and she is at home with little ones (a rare couple in this day!). You return, having used 22,000 of your words. She has only spoke 3,000 of hers, mainly "Stop that!" "Eat that!" and "Take a nap!" She has 22,000 words left to use when you finally arrive at home, and you are the only person in sight for her to spend them on.

It's possible to be in her *company* without being her *companion*. You may feel a mental drift when you come home. You may be Mr. Multitasker with a hundred projects being solved in your mind at any one time. She sits down trying to have intimate conversation with you. Your head shakes up and down, but you're not listening. Finally, you ask her a question and she says, "I just told you that three minutes ago." The truth is, you were not focused on her, not listening to her, not treating her as a special person.

She married you for companionship, to be someone she could talk to about intelligent things, her dreams, and her difficulties. She doesn't want her husband to only be a problem solver. Men like to fix things. They like to solve problems like fixing a leaky faucet or building an addition. Those are great things and are part of your role. The problem is, your wife needs more from you than fixing things. She needs your love, which involves listening and companionship. When she starts into a sentence or two of a problem or frustration, don't cut her off with a three-part solution! Without genuine companionship, over time, the warm, gushing romantic feelings she had at the beginning of your marriage become cold and dried up. She is resentful because it seems that she is nothing more than a roommate or a sex object.

I highly recommend the book *The Seven Levels of Intimacy* by Matthew Kelly. This *New York Times* best-seller says that married couples have conversations on different levels. Most of us spend the majority of our time on the lowest level of conversation—the weather, what happened on the job, and so on. But there are higher levels available: opinions, dreams, fears, and more. Turn off the TV, computer, and cell phone. Take long walks together where you listen to all she has to say, not just cut her off to "fix it."

Years ago, one of my friends and his wife were on their thirtieth-anniversary trip. The first morning, they ordered breakfast in bed and began to talk about their whole lives, their kids, their mistakes, their thrills. When they looked at the clock, it was 4:30 in the afternoon and they were still in their pajamas. They were so overdue on intimate conversation that it took them eight hours to catch up.

How about your wife? Could she use a makeover where you focus on her as much as you did when you dated? Would she faint if you took her overnight somewhere and told her you just wanted to have time to talk and catch up? When your wife perceives that you truly love quality, alone, intimate time with her more than anything else in the world, she'll begin to open up like a *flourishing* flower because you've created a safe space for her. At that point, Mama gets real happy.

If you are like most men, this is one area you'll be working on for life, particularly during seasons when you are incredibly busy. However, just having the knowledge of her deep desire to share her life with you on a daily and hourly basis will put the zing back into your fling.

3. LACK OF ROUTINE

Interruptions make a wife unhappy. When she finally does have you to herself, inevitably someone will text, call, or knock on the door. If you don't have some solid boundaries with other people and learn to say no, she'll start feeling that your life is "open for business" twenty-four hours a day and she's second fiddle.

I was in bed one night about 2:00 a.m. when a knock came at the front door. It was a state trooper who told me that someone was at the State Capitol chained to the front door with dynamite around his waist and was holding a machete to his little boy's neck. He was threatening to blow up the capitol building, and he was asking for *me!* I heard Melanie say from our bed, "He's not going!"

I did go, and it turned out to be flares instead of dynamite.

What's the point here? Interruptions trample on routine, and your wife needs to feel a sense of system and regularity to life. Melanie and I get up about 6:00 a.m. and take a two-mile walk together. Then we eat the same cereal every morning. Then we make coffee the same way and sit in our same two chairs and read our Bibles with our big Rhodesian Ridgeback dog at our feet.

It is routine. Mealtimes, devotional times, bedtimes, and family nights all have to become a routine of life that defends itself against interruption. Interruptions *will* happen, but you have to refuse them when you are at home with your wife. If you have to, build a moat around your house with crocodiles in it, but *defend your life from interruption!*

One pastor I know received a call at 3:30 a.m. from a lady in his church, saying, "Pastor, the Lord told me that you have a word for me right now."

He replied, "He does. Go back to bed!" and hung up.

Mama got happy!

4. COMMUNICATION ISSUES

The type of communication I want to address here is different from issue number two (loneliness). It has to do with your wife being able to freely communicate her frustrations or observations about you to you.

A woman needs to respect her husband. Paul said, *"Let the wife see that she respects her husband"* (Ephesians 5:33). Disrespectful, cutting comments about our character will not be well received! We know we have issues that are unresolved in our character, but disrespect goes nowhere toward helping us to change.

However, if your wife is like most, she genuinely wants to talk to you about some things she doesn't like or doesn't respect about you. It may be about home maintenance, driving techniques, or the fact that your breath could kick-start a 747 jet. It could be one of a hundred things that have aggravated her in living with you.

Years ago, I heard an illustration about this that transformed my thinking on times when my character is confronted. If your collar was sticking up in the back of your shirt and a friend came up and adjusted it, you would thank him. He sees something that you can't see, but that everyone else can see. That's the way you have to look at your wife's gentle, respectful "adjustments." She knows you better than anyone on the planet, yet she loves you. She's for you. When you succeed, she succeeds. You have to let her be your mirror in life because she is trying to tell you what scores of other people can see and wonder why you haven't done anything to change.

My biggest problem was defensiveness. When my wife brought out an issue in my character, I could immediately turn it around so that it was really the result of *her* behavior that made me the way I was! In frustrated desperation, she would drop the subject, and I would go away like a good defense attorney—case closed.

Don't be defensive!

Let your wife adjust you.

If Pilate had listened to his wife about Jesus, he would not have taken his life later over the guilt of what he did that day. God provides your wife to be your helper and your partner. She can make you a far better man than you are right now (see Genesis 2:18). So the next time she tells you that you have been leaving the shower light on all day and night, admit it, apologize, and change.

I'm talking about real, serious change, a thoughtful focus on adjusting the issues that she has finally gotten up her courage to talk to you about. When you do, she will feel validated and that you love her enough to do whatever it takes. Plus, it will make you a better man. Socrates said, "A life unexamined is not worth living!" Let your wife help.

Once again, Mama gets happy.

5. DISHONOR

A couple of years ago, I was in Lagos, Nigeria, doing a conference. There was nothing on television to watch in the hotel except live coverage of Queen Elizabeth's sixtieth anniversary of becoming queen. I happened to turn the TV on when the queen was receiving a special naval honor beside the River Thames. One little lady was sitting on a chair on the riverbank while one thousand ships sailed past her in their finest trim, with their crews saluting as they passed her. Wow!

I have been to the Tower of London and have seen the crown jewels. Elizabeth was twenty-five when she was crowned queen by the archbishop of Canterbury. She received a crown covered in diamonds and a mace with a diamond on top larger than a golf ball! (Trust me, that little thing you gave your wife is not that big of a deal.)

In sixty years, Queen Elizabeth has not opened a door in public or had a driver's license. Men break their necks to get doors open before her in buildings and help her to get into the back of her chauffeur-driven car. As I watched this scene for several days, I realized how little I had honored my wife!

I watch guys walking ten feet in front of their wives. They are oblivious to where she even is. When she walks into a room, they don't even look up. When they approach a door, they let themselves through and let it fall back on her.

One of my dear friends, Billy Hornsby, was a state trooper and founder of ARC, a church-planting organization.

When I was twenty-three, I watched how Billy treated his wife, Charlene. He would open every door before her. He walked alongside her like he was escorting the queen of the world. He would walk around to her side of the car to open the door and help her into her seat. His example transformed my life!

Billy recently passed away (as did his beautiful wife, Charlene), but when he was on his deathbed, I promised him that I would tell the world about how he had honored his wife.

So I want you, as a *model man*, to walk beside your wife, opening every door in front of her. When you walk to the parking lot, go around to her side, open her door, and (after you pick her up from the ground, where she fainted), help her to get into the passenger seat.

Treat her like she's the queen of the world, *"showing honor to the woman as the weaker vessel ...that your prayers may not be hindered"* (1 Peter 3:7). The way you are honoring (or dishonoring) your wife could be affecting the way your prayers are being answered by God.

Dress her well. Get her a nice, safe car. Go out of your way to show her respect and honor...and watch Mama get *real* happy.

6. MISTRUST

Trust is critical in a marriage.

A wife needs to feel transparency and honesty from her husband. If he is shady, manipulative, and unethical, she loses respect. This is one area I have not struggled in, but I feel it is critical to bring it out.

Go back to chapter 1 ("Courageous Integrity") and review those thoughts. A *model man* keeps his word to his wife. He keeps his commitments, even the simple ones like promising to be home at 5:00 for dinner.

You must be a man who keeps his distance from every other woman but her.

One wife confided in Melanie that she feels uneasy all the time because her husband flirts with every waitress and stewardess. When a wife becomes uncertain of her husband's total devotion, a deep sadness envelops her life. Make yourself totally accountable to your wife: in financial matters, taxes, travel, and every other dimension of life.

Have no secrets from her.

Never lie to her.

Get over the embarrassment of telling the truth about your mistakes. Melanie knows I am not perfect, but she knows she can trust my word to her as being 100 percent accurate for our entire life.

7. UNPROTECTED

This last mistake came to me as I was in an extended time of seeking the Lord. I heard God's still, small voice as clearly as I've ever heard it in my life. He said to me, "You are not covering your wife."

I did not even know what that meant. Immediately, though, a passage from the book of Ruth came into my mind.

Boaz, Ruth's nearest redeemer, was sleeping on his threshing floor, and she lay down on the floor at the end of his bed. He woke up in the night and asked, "Who are you?"

She replied, *"I am Ruth your maid. So spread your covering over your maid"* (Ruth 3:9, NASB).

Boaz represented protection from danger, want, and destitution. Ruth needed a "covering," one who would step between her and the broken life she was facing without him.

Immediately I realized my problem. A woman wants to be covered, but I was leaving Melanie to fend for herself! At home, at church, and in the store, I did not protect her from anything awkward or difficult in her life. At this realization, I called her into our bedroom and asked for her forgiveness. Her big blue eyes blinked with tears as I told her what I had discovered.

From that day until now, whenever she doesn't know what to do in a situation, she whispers, "Cover me." Whether it is with church members, neighbors, school officials, or even our own children who have disrespected her, I step between her and the problem. If a neighbor knocks on the door with an accusation about our child, I answer the door. If a caller is abusive on the phone, she hands me the receiver and I say in a deep male voice, "Do you have a problem, or are you looking for a problem?"

Policemen cover your home at night. They watch for intruders as they patrol the neighborhood. Policemen don't control your life. They don't go inside your home and raid your pantry whenever they want to. They respect your privacy and property, yet they are prepared to leap from their car at a moment's notice with guns pulled when they see a stranger entering your window.

Like the police, *cover* your wife; don't *smother* her. Give her space to blossom and flourish while you cover her.

I want to conclude this point with a real-life story that happened to one of our Surge Project directors in Rio de Janeiro, Brazil. One night, two gunmen made their way into Philip and Renee Murdoch's home in suburban Rio. They demanded that Philip give them the $50,000 he supposedly had in his bedroom. Philip adamantly told them that he did not have any money in his room.

Then one of the men decided to threaten Philip's wife. "If you don't get that money, we are going to rape your wife."

Philip stepped between the gun and his wife and said, "If you touch my wife, one of us is going to die right here and right now."

The man backed down and eventually left their home with a few goods and a threat of coming back if Philip told the police.

You should hear Renee tell the story: "Philip is my hero!" When it was all on the line, at crunch time, Philip covered his wife.

You see, that's all she needs to know, that you are guarding her, protecting her, willing to lay down your life, if necessary, to defend her. One of my favorite movie scenes is Harrison Ford throwing the terrorist off the back of Air Force One and saying, "Get off of my plane!" In your mind, you are saying to any person who would attack your precious wife, "Back off from *my wife!*"

Mama is going to stay happy.

I hope these seven mistakes that I've made in my marriage will help you to correct the areas that you are struggling with in yours. If you want to be a *model man*, it all starts at home. If you will give your wife financial security, companionship, routine, communication, honor, trust, and protection, she will love you for the rest of your life.

In the next chapter, we'll look at another relationship where your leadership, example, and ability to stay connected in relationships will have implications for your entire life: raising your children.

DISCUSSION QUESTIONS

1. Financial insecurity causes a high percentage of divorces. What steps have you taken to assure your wife that her future is financially secure?

2. Would you say you suffer from being distracted at home by work, hobbies, and projects? How has it affected the companionship between you and your wife?

3. When is the last time your wife confronted you over your character or behavior, and how did you respond?

4. Your wife married you to be honored and protected. Does she feel that from you when you are in public together?

RAISING UP SONS AND DAUGHTERS

And you, fathers, do not provoke your children
to wrath, but bring them up in the training
and admonition of the Lord. —EPHESIANS 6:4

ABSENT, ANONYMOUS, ABUSIVE

Our nation is reaping the results of a fatherless generation. Children are growing up with holes in their hearts. Young boys are becoming men without any sense of identity or confidence. Young girls are giving themselves away for cheap because they have never been honored by a father. Listen to these sobering statistics:

- 75 percent of all adolescent patients in chemical abuse centers come from fatherless homes—10 times the average.

- 71 percent of all high school dropouts come from fatherless homes—9 times the average.

- 80 percent of rapists with anger problems come from fatherless homes—14 times the average (*Criminal Justice and Behavior*, vol. 14, 403-26).

- 85 percent of all children who show behavior disorders come from fatherless homes—20 times the average (Centers for Disease Control).

- 90 percent of all homeless and runaway children are from fatherless homes—32 times the average.

- 70 percent of youths in state-operated institutions come from fatherless homes—9 times the average (US Department of Justice).

- 85 percent of all youths in prison come from fatherless homes—20 times the average (Fulton County, Georgia; Texas Department of Corrections)

- 71 percent of pregnant teenagers lack a father (US Department of Health and Human Services).[1]

Had enough? I could go on, but I think you get the picture. Fathering shapes a nation, either positively or negatively. Don't you think we've had enough of the negative? It's time for fathers to become *model men* and step up to the plate! We can turn this thing around and reshape the next generation, and the generations after that.

As I have said, I have six children (five sons and a daughter), who are all serving God and involved in ministry. My sons' spouses are godly, pure women who serve Christ and their families with all their hearts. Our grandchildren are growing up in stable, disciplined, loving, joyful homes.

Does it get any better? No wonder the psalmist said:

> *Behold, children are a heritage from the Lord,*
> *the fruit of the womb a reward.*
> *Like arrows in the hands of a warrior*
> *are the children of one's youth.*
> *Blessed is the man*
> *who fills his quiver with them!*
> (Psalm 127:3-5)

We all make mistakes with our children. I've made some huge ones. None of our children has had a perfect life. I attribute the deep mistakes my children have made to a gaping hole in my own fathering. You can even be a great father and have children drift away from the Lord (look at the prodigal son). I promise you, though, that if you will do the *three* things in this chapter, your family *will* turn around. It may take months or years, but mistakes can turn into miracles!

Let's look at three broad areas that contain a lot of fathering techniques in raising successful sons and daughters.

1. ATTENTION

A little boy kept trying to get his dad's attention as Dad was hidden behind his newspaper. Finally he brought a nickel to his father.

His dad said, "What's this?"

The little boy replied, "Is this enough to buy an hour of your time?"

Spend at least fifteen minutes a day in undisturbed conversation with each child. There, I said it.

You may say, "I don't have fifteen minutes a day."

Then perhaps you should not have had children.

Children cannot hold in their feelings, their disappointments, or hurts of the day for fifteen minutes. When you say, "How was your day?" and a child says, "Okay" (but you can sense that it really was not okay), in about ten minutes of probing, the tears will begin to roll.

You cannot pass your children mindlessly in your home like ships passing in the harbor. They are growing deeper and deeper into themselves, their problems, their anger, their shame. It takes time to release those feelings, and you are the one to give it.

For me, with six children, that was an hour and a half a day. I hit my goal most days, sometimes only finishing up late at night sitting by their bedside. Even today, when they are grown, I have the sensation of wanting to be with each of them equally every day.

Follow practices that show your children that you are interested in everything that affects them.

Get involved with what they are involved in. The only way to pay attention is to participate in the things they are interested in. I failed to do this with one of my sons. He begged me to play a particular sport with him, but I had no interest in it. Unbeknownst to me, he developed a relationship with some errant friends while playing that sport, and Dad was nowhere around.

I almost lost him because of that mistake.

I hate paintball. I got shot in the ear once with a paintball (I think it is still ringing). However, one of my sons loved it for a season when he was young. Thank the Lord he grew out of it! But by then I had learned my lesson well.

For your child, attention is looking over when they are doing their favorite thing and seeing Dad right there beside them.

Monitor all relationships. In today's world, relationships can blossom overnight. A texting "relationship" can exist between someone and your child without you ever meeting or even seeing the person. One of my children "fell in love" (at fourteen) as a result of a texting relationship. I discovered his phone and saw the words *love* and *baby*. I called him in, and that was the end of that.

You may think that because your child is in a Christian school, all his or her relationships are Christian. Wrong! You may think that every child on your street is harmless and pure. Wrong! We always had children come over to *our* house instead of letting our children spend hours a day at *their* houses. Since most molestation happens in sleepover situations where a friend or cousin is present, we never let our children spend the night elsewhere. "You have all day to play until you are worn out," we would say. "Go to your own homes and sleep; then hit it again in the morning."

I believe you should instill in your children from an early age the understanding that you will help them find their spouse. Who besides their parents knows them better and can better discern the type of personality they will be able to coexist with for a lifetime? When our children were little, I would tell them, "When you grow up, you are going to fall in love." They would laugh hysterically at this, but I would go on: "Daddy and Mama will help you find just the perfect person to marry." They would nod their heads with wide eyes.

You know what? It worked. For each of our sons and our daughter, we have helped them navigate through the personality style, character, family background, and compatibility of their potential spouses. Several times we've had to say, "No go."

I'm sort of like the chimpanzee in the Disney movie *Barefoot Executive*. This chimp could watch TV and respond to a program by clapping his hands or wagging his head back and forth from side to side. His response could predict national TV ratings perfectly. That was me. When a relationship reached a stage of becoming serious, our children would ask us what we thought, and I would give them the clapped hands or the wagged head!

We saved each of them from several obviously wrong relationships that their emotions had blinded them to. They have each married a spouse fitted to their demeanor and compatible with their calling.

Have a family night. I spoke about this during the chapter on discipline. I consider having a family night to be perhaps the most important thing you can do in parenting.

What it says to a child is "You are important. I put no one ahead of you. Your place in my life is above my work, my friends, and my hobbies. I may have to correct you plenty during the week, but tonight is a night for just plain fun."

I allowed each child to have a night when he or she was able to direct some of the activities (based on the child's favorite thing to do). Sometimes we'd watch movies together and pop popcorn or make pizza. Sometimes we played charades. We always wrestled on the floor and tickled. I was the "doctor" tickling them by operating on each of them by "sawing" on their back or "sawing" off a leg. Their favorite was when I played a particular happy song on the piano while they laid on their backs and did an imaginary bicycle (the fastest bicycle would win). We played chase in the house where I hid from them as the "wolf." We did tumbling with all the furniture moved back so I could flip them over my head while I lay flat on the floor.

You get it? *Fun.* Imagine how I feel now when I see one of my sons get on his piano, playing the same fast song, and his little girls get on the floor and do the imaginary bicycle! No wonder their childhood memories always go back to family night.

2. AFFECTION

When Jesus came out of the waters of baptism, God spoke words of affirmation to Him. *"You are my Son, whom I love; with you I am well pleased"* (Mark 1:11, NIV). First,

He gave Him *identity*: *"You are my Son."* Jesus knew He belonged to the Father. Second, the Father gave Jesus *validity*: *"whom I love."* He validated Christ publicly, stating to all that He loved Him. Finally, He gave Him *affirmation*: *"in You I am well pleased."* He told Him personally how proud He was of Him.

Can you see these as the missing ingredients in men today? Nation after nation, wherever I go, people break down and weep when they realize how fatherless they feel.

"Olive plant" children have deep roots in acceptance and affirmation (see Psalm 128:3). They face life with confidence and assurance, hearing for life that inward voice of identity, validity, and affirmation they received from their father. Those who never hear those words spend their lives trying to prove themselves, promote themselves, and pattern themselves after others. They fear every new challenge, inwardly expecting to fail. But Jesus faced His new ministry at thirty with a thunderous affirmation from heaven that rang in His soul until He said, *"It is finished"* from the cross. And your kids can have a similar confidence.

Affection, of course, should be physical. Touch, hugs, and kisses should very much be a part of your home culture. A distant, cold, performance-only culture does not allow the true affirmation and love of God to penetrate it. The prodigal son's father sure got affectionate with him:

"He ran to his son, threw his arms around him and kissed him" (Luke 15:20, NIV).

You may not be a huggy-kissy type of man. At the least, however, you can say, "I love you" and "I'm proud of you" repeatedly throughout your children's lives. I know a well-known leader whose three sons have all struggled with their identities. At his grave, one of them, shaking with emotion and fighting back tears, said to a bystander, "He never once told us that he loved us or that he was pleased with us."

Mart Green of the Hobby Lobby Corporation told me about a valedictorian who gave the most stirring five-minute address in her university's history. (The school would go on to use it everywhere in its recruiting.) Mart was there and was as impressed by her talk as anybody. Afterward, Mart complimented the young woman.

She replied, "I have a hole in my heart."

With a little prompting, she told the story of how she, her brothers, and their single mother lived in poverty after her parents divorced. Her father told her at sixteen years old, "I never want to hear from you again." She faithfully wrote him letters for years during college and never received a response. Eventually she received an envelope with every letter she had ever written him (they were opened) and a note that said, "I told you I never wanted to hear from you again." He was missing on the day of her valedictory triumph.

Is it any wonder we are dealing with such rage, frustration, and fear in the new generation? All they need is a little bit of affirmation.

Be present at every big day. I played basketball in high school. (I was six feet, two inches tall and weighed 135 pounds. If I turned sideways and stuck out my tongue, I looked like a zipper.) I could be playing rather routinely until I noticed the gym door open and a smaller man step in and make his way to the top of the bleachers. Suddenly I played like a being from another world! I blocked shots, made plays, and hit shots from the top of the arc. What was the difference? That small man on the top row was *my dad*.

When children have a game, an award, or any type of performance, they are looking around for *you*. I know you are busy, but will you ever be able to replace not being there once they are grown and gone? What was it that was so important in your life that you could not tell them it had to wait? I have rejoiced to see golf pros who have missed whole tournaments because one of their children had a big day somewhere.

I remember the big day of one of my sons. He had had a rough time in college, had fallen in with the wrong crowd, and had dropped out after having been a 4.0

student at one point. When he came back to the Lord, he fearfully enrolled at a college several states away, asking me, "Dad, do you think I have what it takes to make it in college again?"

I said, "Yes, you have it. You are going to do great."

Great he did. I hardly remember a test that he made lower than a 98 on in two and a half years.

Our family was going to his graduation several weeks away, a big expense for airfares and hotels. Then I heard that he was being honored at a chapel for Student of the Year. I quickly made a second flight reservation without telling him and showed up in the back of the school auditorium the day of the award.

The dean of the business school gave many accolades and ended with these words: "In fifteen years as dean of this college, I have never had a better student than this one." He went on to tell about my son's accomplishments and attitude; then he put a huge medal around his neck.

I bolted for the side doors where my boy was leaving when it was over. In the lobby, I caught him as he was just pushing the doors open to leave. I called his name, and he whirled around. Can I tell you that tears *shot* from his eyes!

He said, "Dad, I was so hoping you would be here to hear those things they were saying about me."

I said, "I heard every word, son," and we hugged each other through tears, celebrating the huge victory in his life.

There it is right there. Remember, Dad, no one can affirm your child like you.

Discipline. One of the greatest books I have ever read is *Boundaries with Kids* by Henry Cloud and John Townsend. I highly recommend you get that book to help you with the discipline of your children. It outlines the two principles you need to know to remain in control of the discipline and upbringing of your children: *boundaries* and *consequences.*

They describe how God, the perfect parent, used the tree of the knowledge of good and evil in the Bible as His "boundary." He told Adam and Eve that they were free to eat of every tree in the garden except that one. In essence, He drew a line around it as off-limits. Then He clearly outlined the consequences of eating the fruit: *"When you eat of it, you will surely die"* (Genesis 2:17, NIV).

Why are parents so helpless in controlling their children? They use anger, calling them by their middle names, reasoning, and even abusive language and actions as they try to stare down little Johnny who is throwing peas at the table. I have always been amazed that a 30-pound two-year-old could have total leverage over a 230-pound man!

What did God do? The moment the first couple crossed the boundary in disobedience, He called Adam's name. He reminded Adam and Eve of His command and their bad choice. Then, when they repented, He clothed them in the garments of animals as a sign of atonement of their sin. You will notice, however, the most important thing God did: *He followed through on His consequences by removing them from the garden.*

The simple application is that in order to discipline children, you start with a clear session where you give them the boundaries about doing chores, choosing friends, going places, and a host of behaviors you as a parent want them to comply with. Then you clearly spell out the consequences: loss of privilege (media, outings, events), loss of property (car keys, skateboards, cell phones), or even spanking and a host of other leverages available to you as the parent in charge. Then you let them make their choices.

Good choices mean good consequences. Bad choices mean bad consequences. The moment they make a bad choice, you enforce the consequences, regardless of their wailing, anger, protest, manipulation, holding their breath, or any other method of getting past the pain.

The author of Hebrews wrote, *"No discipline seems pleasant at the time, but painful. Later on, however, it produces a harvest of righteousness and peace for those who have been trained by it"* (Hebrews 12:11, NIV). This verse teaches that pain changes character.

Cloud and Townsend remind us that it is simply God's law of sowing and reaping. Whenever I, as a parent, interfere with this principle so that my child never reaps the consequence of his or behavior (because I never want the child to feel any pain), I have precluded God's way to change a person's character!

Never step between a disobedient act and the consequence. If your child experiences consequences for his behavior at school, on the highway, or in breaking any law, let the consequences happen. Don't bail him out until you have seen the true fruits of repentance: "I deserve this. I am going to change." If you remove him from that pain prematurely, you may never have another opportunity to change his character.

Remember that children are most teachable between ages 0 and 5. You have to win the battle of the will during those ages. The concrete is still wet during those most important 250 weekends. Carefully focus on every sinful, rebellious, willful character trait that surfaces: lying, anger, destructive behavior, jealousy, disruption, theft, or whatever it may be.

Establish good habits in your children's lives from the time they are small.

- Order—their bedroom, their clothes, their bathroom.

- Devotion to God—daily time in reading the Bible, first with you and then on their own, attending church with you.

- Work—doing simple chores every day and rotating in kitchen, clothes folding, and yard work.

- Punctuality—getting up and going to bed on time (when *you* say), ready for school and meals.

- Respect—honoring teachers, police, pastors, the elderly, and any person who carries authority in their lives.

- Time management—limited video games, television, social media, any hobby that consumes them in a world where they lose track of time.

- Money management—tithing their allowance and income, learning to save, taking care of possessions so they don't have to be replaced.

- Manners—table manners, addressing adults, dressing appropriately for events.

We often ate at restaurants as a family. Almost always, someone would approach me as we were leaving and say, "How did you do that? How did your children sit there at the table and eat like normal people?"

I told them about my eyebrow.

I can raise my left eyebrow and leave the other one flat. It transforms my face from calm into a very fearsome look! When one of my kids decided to throw peas across the table, I called his name. When he looked at me, I raised that eyebrow. In that one look were these words: "If you don't cease in your operation and desist in your maneuver, when we get home, there won't be enough comic books to stuff into the seat of your blue jeans when I apply the 'board of education' to the 'seat of higher learning.'"

It's all in the eyebrow.

←———————●———————→

From this day forward, start looking at your children differently. See in them a future professor, president, and steward of all the resources you accumulate in your lifetime. Train them as the best possible manager and ultimately replacement of you in the world. That is your legacy, and it is the final chapter of a life that begins with integrity.

DISCUSSION QUESTIONS

1. Did you have a surprise about one of your children lately in his conduct or relationships? What made you take your eye off the ball?

2. Have you showered your children with affirmation, proving it by being there at their big days? How did your father treat you that is somehow keeping you from being able to treat your children with affection?

3. Do your children really know their boundaries at home, in town, with other children, and at school?

4. Do you bat a thousand with enforcing consequences when your kids step over the line?

NOTE

1. The Fatherless Generation: Statistics, http://thefatherlessgeneration.wordpress.com/statistics/.

LEGACY...YOUR HIGHEST ASSIGNMENT

*We have heard and known because our
fathers have told us. We will not hide them
from their children. But we will tell the
children-to-come the praises of the Lord,
and of His power and the great things
He has done.* —PSALM 78:3-4, NLT

CONGRATULATIONS! YOU'VE HUNG in there and
made it to the final chapter of this journey. Along the
way, God has changed your *character,* challenged your
consistency, and *restored* your relationships. Now there is
only one thing left: your legacy.

A legacy is something handed down, passed on to the
next generation. It has to do with mentoring, the intentional shaping of another person to carry your values and
vision after you are gone.

Elijah is a perfect example of a mentor. He reached a point in his life where calling down fire, killing false prophets, and hiding from Ahab was no longer his passion. He ran from Jezebel, looking for meaning and new purpose. In the cave at Sinai, he saw the wind, the earthquake, and the fire (see 1 Kings 19:11-13). Suddenly the Lord spoke to him in a *"gentle whisper,"* giving instructions: *"Elisha the son of Shaphat of Abel-meholah you shall anoint to be prophet in your place"* (verse 16).

In your place? Elijah may have thought. *Could God's kingdom go on without me?*

We, too, may think, *Is it possible that I am a link in a chain of the kingdom of God, useful in my lifetime, but especially useful to God in how I transfer my gifts to the next generation? Why should I not just keep doing my thing until my final breath, then expire and let God raise up someone else?*

The kingdom of God is like a chain or a relay race. The linking of generations and runners is how you received the gospel in the first place. Mentoring and discipleship of others is the *baton*, and passing it on should rank as your highest assignment in your lifetime.

Paul said to the Romans, *"I long to see you, that I may impart to you some spiritual gift to strengthen you—that is, that we may be mutually encouraged by each other's faith, both yours and mine"* (Romans 1:11-12). His greatest desire was to impart to others, and watching them develop was his greatest fulfillment.

Jesus took only three short years to disciple eleven men who in turn changed all of history (this is that inner circle we talked about under "pace" in chapter 4). It's going to take you time, effort, energy, and money to fashion a leader, a successor, a Joshua who can lead Israel where you as Moses have not been allowed to go.

While ministering in the Philippines, Bill Bright mentored one man and his wife. That couple eventually went back to their native Thailand and over a six-year period won seven hundred people to the Lord. Those seven hundred led ninety thousand to the Lord, and no one can even trace how many those ninety thousand won and discipled to Christ...*from one man.*[1]

Legacy is the process by which God takes your *character, consistency*, and *connections* to transfer kingdom values to the next generation. Legacy is about raising up "sons."

PAUL AND TIMOTHY

As far as we know, Paul had no biological sons, but he had many spiritual sons.

In Lystra and Derbe (in modern-day Turkey), Paul found Timothy, a young man who impressed him as having real character and love for God. Timothy's mother was Jewish, and his father was Greek (see Acts 16:1). We don't know exactly what Paul saw in this young man, but it was enough to ask him to accompany him on his missionary journey.

I have been to Turkey and Greece and have seen some of the remains of the Roman road system that passed through all parts of the Roman world. These roads were amazing. The most elaborate were more than a yard thick and up to seven yards wide, allowing chariots to pass each other easily, often with sidewalks and mile markers. Every twenty miles, there were typically an inn and a military outpost. There were over fifty thousand miles of these roads across the vast Roman Empire.

Paul walked those roads daily with Timothy. In fact, the New Testament records at least eighteen young men whom Paul picked for his team during his travels. As they walked a day's journey (around twenty miles), I'm sure these young men talked, discussed, and learned from the greatest apostle of all time.

Timothy was Paul's closest and dearest spiritual son. Timothy demonstrated the greatest hunger and desire for spiritual things. He loved the churches Paul planted like Paul himself did. Listen to a few verses that describe Paul's relationship to this young man, and see what they can teach you about being a model to a younger man.

1. A son is a friend. Paul wrote to the Corinthians, *"I am sending to you Timothy, **my son whom I love**, who is* *faithful in the Lord. He will remind you of my way of life in Christ Jesus, which agrees with what I teach everywhere in every church"* (First Corinthians 4:17, NIV, emphasis added). These two were clearly very close.

A son has to be with you enough for your way of life, attitude, and perspective to wear off on him. The passing of legacy comes from rubbing shoulders with a father, listening, observing, and emulating his way of life. Therefore, your own children will be your greatest spiritual sons. Other "sons" will also be greatly affected by your life, but don't count out the power of a lifetime of discipleship of your own children.

Having five sons and a daughter, I have seen what the day-in and day-out lifestyle of serving God in our home and family produced in them. They know how I think, how to react to situations, how to steer clear of danger and temptation, how to work, and, of course, how to seek the Lord. It's a blessing to sit back now and watch them do things in an even better way than I did them, marveling that they carry my values with their vision.

Mentoring is spelled T-I-M-E.

It is not a lesson or a lecture; it is a lifestyle.

Mentoring is hanging out together, traveling together, listening, sharing, and being there when they are going through a struggle. You say you are too busy to mentor sons? You may turn out like Absalom: *"Absalom in his lifetime had taken and set up for himself the pillar that is in the King's Valley, for he said, 'I have no son to keep my name in remembrance'"* (2 Samuel 18:18).

Because Absalom was not a *mentor*, he had to make a *monument*. A street named after you, or a plaque on a company wall is not your legacy. Your legacy is a son, an heir, a leader who has been shaped by your leadership.

2. A son is a servant. On another occasion, Paul wrote again about Timothy: *"I have no one else like him, who takes a genuine interest in your welfare. For everyone looks out for his own interests, not those of Jesus Christ. But you know that Timothy has proved himself,* **because as a son with his father** *he has served with me in the work of the gospel"* (Philippians 2:20-22, NIV, emphasis added).

Paul was a worker. He made tents as a journeyman. He supported himself for years. He was no stranger to hard work. Anyone who wanted to be his apprentice, his son, his successor, would have to be a young man who loved the ministry as much as Paul.

Years ago, a guy applied to be a pastor on our staff (we had twenty-eight pastors at the time). After he filled out the application, the secretary asked him if he would mind going into the mailroom and stapling together two stacks of papers that needed stapling while they processed his application. "I don't staple papers" was his reply.

Little did he know that it was part of our process for ministry to see if someone would be willing to do the most menial job regardless of his training and title. This man's application process was completed the moment he said that!

My dad is a worker. He loved mowing, grading, painting, sweeping, constructing anything that was going on around the church property. He didn't have much patience for sitting in an office. One day, a young man came up looking for the pastor. He saw a man painting on a ladder and asked him for directions. "You are looking at him. Grab a brush and we can talk while we paint," my dad replied.

Something about Timothy really fit with Paul. Here was a young man who loved to work hard, loved people as Paul did, and seemed to have a sterling character. He *served with* Paul, interested in any project Paul was doing and willing to help on any mission Paul wanted to send him on.

3. A son is a mentor himself. There is still another verse that teaches us about mentoring. Paul writes to Timothy, *"You then, my son, be strong in the grace that is in Christ Jesus. And the things you have heard me say in the presence of many witnesses entrust to reliable men who will also be qualified to teach others"* (2 Timothy 2:1-2, NIV, emphasis added).

Now we are talking about *grandchildren!*

What greater joy is there in life than a grandchild? If you've lived long enough to have them (as I have), they are your greatest joy. You love them—and you can leave them when you want to!

What a fulfillment to see one of your children having children and raising them up in the godly values you imparted to him or her. The satisfaction is incredible.

Recently our church celebrated its fiftieth anniversary at a huge service in the civic center in Baton Rouge. The name of the service was Legacy Lives. What a celebration it was! My father, Roy Stockstill, founded our church in our living room with a handful of people when I was ten years old and in the fourth grade. For the anniversary service, he stood at ninety-four years of age and greeted the vast crowd, rejoicing in God's goodness and grace to have multiplied our church to many thousands. Then Melanie and I stood and greeted this great congregation that we pastored for twenty-eight years. Finally, my son Jonathan and his wife, Angie, ministered to the group, having pastored now for two years.

Legacy did indeed live that night.

I'm giving you a picture of your future. God is going to give you spiritual and natural children who will receive your godly character and consistency and impart it to their generation and generations beyond. I don't know what you are thinking is important, but believe me, *that* is the most important!

JESUS AND HIS DISCIPLES

There was no better mentor who left a longer legacy than Jesus Christ. His disciples multiplied into every nation, every culture, and every generation. Amazingly, it all started with eleven good men.

How did He do it? I've got four words for you: *selection, impartation, confrontation,* and *commitment.*

1. Selection. Jesus chose those He would leave His legacy with carefully. He chose men who were active go-getters with something already going on in their world. From Peter and John fishing to Levi tax collecting, they were engaged in the business and working world. It reminds me of Elijah finding Elisha in the field plowing with twelve yoke of oxen (see 1 Kings 19:19).

Your world is full of good men who could use a little direction and impartation. They need someone who will believe in them. They are not looking for a handout, but a hand up. They are making the most of what they can do with the resources they have.

2. Impartation. Jesus had intentionality about the men He chose. He preferred to be with them even more than with the multitudes. This group ate together, slept in the fields together, healed the sick together, passed out bread together, and walked the dusty roads of Israel together.

You can't escape this second principle of Jesus' mentoring. You are going to have to become intentional about mentoring others. Take them with you to do whatever you do: hunting and fishing, going to ball games, eating out, rebuilding an engine block. Do life together.

3. Confrontation. Now, here comes the big one. Can the person you are mentoring take a little correction, receiving it like a championship quarterback being shaped by a coach?

Jesus obviously had no problem confronting His team. For example, one day He confronted all of them about arguing over who was the greatest. He brought a little child into the circle as an object lesson and taught them that the greatest must become like a child (see Mark 9:33-37).

Everyone remembers when He confronted Peter by saying, *"Get away from me, Satan! …You are seeing things merely from a human point of view, not from God's"* (Matthew 16:23, NLT).

The more time you spend with a person, the more likely it is that attitudes needing confrontation will surface. That's okay. That's part of mentoring.

Without confrontation, there is no change.

Without change, there is no champion.

David was a great king of Israel, but not a very good father. He had an unbroken, headstrong son named Adonijah, who eventually rose up and tried to take away the kingdom. Notice David's mistake: *"His father, King David, had never disciplined him at any time, even by asking, 'Why are you doing that?'"* (1 Kings 1:6, NLT). What David refused to confront eventually rose up to try to destroy him.

I believe that a hand on the shoulder and a question like "Why are you doing that?" can change the direction of someone you are mentoring. It is challenging his over-confidence, selfishness, inconsistency, or wrong attitudes.

I played athletics all my life and had some pretty successful coaches. Those coaches were the ones who focused intensely on the wrong moves, bad shooting form, and wrong habits that could lose a game in the final seconds. I was thankful for such a good coach because he always brought my game to the next level and added value to me as a player by his continual confrontation of bad habits.

You cannot tolerate bad character in someone you mentor. In a pressure situation, it could destroy him and others if he has power and authority given to him. In love, you simply ask the question "Now tell me. Why did you do that?"

4. Commitment. Believe it or not, Jesus had disciples who walked away from Him. He had to ask His team, *"Are you also going to leave?"* (John 6:66-67, NLT).

Those you select, spend time with, and lovingly confront may reach a moment of either going forward in their relationship with you or backing out. Christ was not afraid of that moment, always leaving the door open for those who felt that the heat in the kitchen was a little too hot.

The story is told that Alexander the Great arrived on the shores of Persia to face the most formidable naval fleet in the world. The Greeks were far outnumbered by the Persians. Alexander, however, gave the command "Burn the boats." There would be no retreat or exit strategy. They would win the war and go home in the boats of their enemies, or they would die.

Elisha *"returned to his oxen and slaughtered them. He used the wood from the plow to build a fire to roast their flesh…. Then he went with Elijah as his assistant"* (1 Kings 19:21, NLT). There it is. No going back. No retreat. It's a total commitment to a mentoring relationship and to carrying a torch forward into the next generation.

YOUR LEGACY

Now we come to the point of this book.

Our nation is in trouble.

Random acts of violence by young, angry males are filling our culture with fear and anxiety. Did you know that none of the mass murders has been carried out by a woman?

The prophet Malachi ended the entire Old Testament with this phrase: *"His preaching will turn the hearts of fathers to their children, and the hearts of children to their fathers. Otherwise I will come and strike the land with a curse"* (Malachi 4:6, NLT).

The curse is here.

Our nation is out of control.

A fatherless generation is lashing out at those who spurned them, those who spoiled them. Without discipline, there is no restraint. A godless generation, caught up in the imaginary world of video, has little regard for life or property.

Somebody has to step away from the cadence of work, money, property, and position and begin to realize that we are losing our culture. Instead of thinking only of retirement, the "me generation" that I am a part of has to wake up and turn around to the next generation.

Here are three guidelines if you are ready to wake up:

Recognize the members of the next generation as important. They must feel that they are not only being *tolerated,* but also being *developed.* Give them a place at your table, at your platform. Introduce them to others as a protégé, one whose training or career is promoted by an influential person.

Give them some "wheel time." Surely you remember when your first child got a driver's license. It was one thing to let this youngster steer on an empty parking lot and quite another to let him or her steer on a highway. "Wheel time" gives confidence. Bring the men you mentor into whatever you are doing and give them a turn. Guide them through their mistakes and reinforce their victories with the valuable input they crave from someone further along in life.

Give them some mercy. Mentoring takes patience. Don't allow one major mistake someone else makes to disqualify him in your mind. Think back to some of the dumb things you did in life! When a person falls from a horse, getting back on the saddle quickly saves him from a lifetime of limitation.

──────●──────

Do you remember when someone taught you to ride a bike? The first few pedals as the front wheel wobbled back and forth and you ended up in a bush? Your parent running alongside the bike, out of breath, trying to steady you as you gained confidence with every push of the pedals? The first few seconds when your parent took his hands off and you pedaled alone? Your giddy excitement when you realized you were riding a bike all by yourself?

Now think about the moment you looked back over your shoulder an hour later and saw the satisfied parent with his hands on his hips, smiling from ear to ear. Years later, when bicycling was second nature, you could hardly remember that feeling of awkward, fearful motion on day one.

That smiling parent is you. That child on the bike is your legacy. At the end of your life, you will scan the horizon around you and see people everywhere riding bikes that you taught them to ride. You will teach them *character, consistency,* and *connection.* You will teach them what you learned in this book and more. You will change your nation because you have changed yourself.

Let's go!

DISCUSSION QUESTIONS

1. In our generation, men are thinking less and less about their legacy and more and more about themselves. Why is it important to starting thinking *right now* about the next generation that will succeed you?

2. Paul had Timothy, his dear son in the faith. Tradition says that Timothy took over Paul's largest congregation, in Ephesus. Who are you grooming right now who has the potential to go beyond your achievements?

3. Jesus was not afraid to confront His disciples. How are loving correction and confrontation the heart and soul of good coaching?

4. We all would rather do it ourselves than give the inexperienced a chance. What can you do better to give others an opportunity to do what you do so you can mentor them to excel you?

NOTE

1. Bill Bright, *5 Steps to Making Disciples* (Peachtree City, GA: New Life Publications, 1997), 7-8.

Conclusion

GATHERING AROUND THE TABLE

*And they continued steadfastly in the apostles' doctrine and **fellowship**, in the breaking of bread, and in **prayers**.*
—ACTS 2:42, emphasis added

FIVE YEARS AGO, I started a small group for business leaders. We had eight to ten men there for breakfast, teaching, and discussion. We fit at one large circular table. Now that one table has become twenty-four! Each Wednesday at noon, up to two hundred men meet in the same format. Occasionally I have to miss because of traveling abroad or across America. Even so, the group never seems to fluctuate. It doesn't matter who's presenting the lesson because they have entered into deep, strong relationships with each other.

I believe in the table. As the early church broke *"bread in their homes, they received their food with glad and generous hearts"* (Acts 2:46). Much of Jesus' discipleship was done at a table—Zacchaeus, Matthew, and the disciples who traveled to Emmaus come to mind.

At the businessmen's group, first we have a *meal.* If you study Scripture, you know that breaking bread together (not just taking the Lord's Supper) is a statement of fellowship and covenant. Laban and Jacob settled their hostilities, and Jacob *"called his kinsmen to eat bread"* (Genesis 31:54). God even had a meal with the Jewish elders at Mount Sinai as *"they beheld God, and ate and drank"* (Exodus 24:11). Eternity itself will begin with the *"marriage supper of the Lamb"* (Revelation 19:9).

So we always start with a meal together. Our staff cooks, and guys drop a small offering in the basket at the center of the table to defray the cost. It always comes out even. The first twenty minutes of the meeting is a time of eating, laughter, fellowship, and interaction. We always end the mealtime with introducing new guests to the entire group.

Then we have a *teaching.* Each teaching is designed to last about twenty minutes but sometimes is preceded by a short testimony or an urgent prayer request.[1]

The last twenty minutes is dedicated to *discussion.* The spiritual food has to be chewed and digested. Some people learn best by memorizing, and some learn best by analyzing. Many, however, learn best by applying. They want to know, *Where do we go from here? What can this do to change my life?*

We always end the one-hour meeting with prayer for those who need it. When we do, it never fails that at table after table, the closing prayer ends with clapping and cheering. It is a sign of victory, camaraderie, and excitement. Over twelve hundred men have attended this business luncheon and asked us to keep them informed by e-mail. Each week, ten to fifteen new guests show up and come back as possible.

Through the five years, men have been through difficulties in their lives. Some have died. One group kept an empty chair for one of their table mates for quite a while after he suddenly passed away. Some have had serious diagnoses, and the group has stood with them for answers to prayer. They come from all denominations and backgrounds, but the common theme is "changing our nation one man at a time."

This is *model man.* I envision small "tables" of men meeting all across our nation. Some will meet in restaurants, some in the workplace, and some in homes or church buildings. The meeting will last for only one hour, even though some may arrive early or stay late for fellowship. The very first lessons the group will go through will be the nine chapters of *Model Man*. We will offer a second path of going through *Model Man* in a six-week video small-group curriculum that covers the highlights of character (two studies), consistency (two studies), and connections (two studies). Finally, the group can continue their experience together for almost a year by going through the fifty *Model Man* Bible studies.

In one year, after completing the lessons, the group will be established. Only God knows how far this multiplication will go before it starts to turn the tide of our nation back to character, consistency, and connection.

It's not an accident that this book fell into your hands. Your wife, your children, your legacy, your pace, your discipline, your purpose, your integrity, your purity, your example are all on the line. Perhaps you feel you have already betrayed your future with your past.

I always go back to Jacob.

Jacob was a wheeler-dealer. He could manipulate his way out of any tight spot. He managed to get his brother's birthright and blessing. Like Houdini, he escaped from his brother's wrath and fled to his father's homeland.

God started in on Jacob's character with Uncle Laban. If you have been a trickster and deceiver, God has a "Laban" waiting right around the corner who is a lot slicker than you! After twenty years of cold, frostbite, hunger, misery, and poor wages, Jacob pulled out in the night with Laban's two daughters.

Finally, Jacob came to Peniel (pronounced pe-NI-ul). I like to say that Jacob came out of denial and into Peniel. He knew that his brother, Esau, was coming to kill him. He tried every manipulation he could to try to stop Esau, but he kept coming. Jacob retreated across the River Jabbok to the mountain of Peniel by himself.

That night, the angel of the Lord wrestled with him. At daybreak, the angel touched his thigh and put it permanently out of joint. When the sun rose, Jacob walked back to meet Esau with a limp. The angel changed his name to Israel, and his drive, manipulation, and trickery were finally broken.

You may be like Jacob. You may carry an inner wound like he did because his father loved Esau more than him. He was outwardly successful but inwardly desperate. The night he met the Lord, something was broken in him, but he was changed.

God wants to change you right now. Jesus met Jacob and He wants to meet you—right here and now, *mano a mano*. Your character flaws, your history, your baggage, your ruined relationships, your bad reputation have all come to the cross.

Bring your mess, your shame, your failures to Jesus Christ and *surrender*. Let His blood cover your past from head to toe, beginning to end. Confess Him as your Lord, your leader, your shepherd. Turn your heart away from darkness, bondage, addiction, and bitterness toward others. Turn to the light of Christ, and call upon His name as the resurrected Lord who is alive and listening to you right now.

That peace you sense is a new nature, the power of grace and forgiveness that has entered your heart and life. Lift your eyes, your heart, and your hands and begin to praise Jesus Christ from the bottom of your heart. Submit to His Word and testify to others without shame or embarrassment.

Last night I heard a pastor give an illustration about Camp Lejeune in North Carolina. With F-16s landing right over the highway next door, startled motorists were often frightened with the scream of the engines landing on the airstrip. Someone put up a billboard that said this: "Pardon the noise. It's only the sound of freedom."

Go ahead and make some noise! Rejoice like the crippled man in Acts 3 who had suddenly been given his legs to walk on after a lifetime of begging. Rejoice like the leper who returned to give Christ thanks and glory after his healing. Rejoice like the father who gave a banquet for his prodigal son who had finally returned home. Heaven rejoices over one sinner who repents, and today it is rejoicing over you!

I pray for you today as you begin a new life, a new start, a new journey. Heaven is our home, and we need each other to get there. It won't happen overnight, but as you grow and develop in the Word of God, one day someone is going to say out of the blue to you:

"You are a model man."

Note

1. As a sequel to this book, we are publishing the *Model Man Bible Studies,* which are fifty of the Bible stories we have done together.

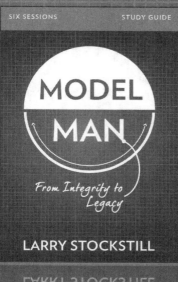

MODEL MAN: STUDY GUIDE
From Integrity to Legacy
by Larry Stockstill

This 6-week *Model Man Study Guide* will help you follow along with Larry Stockstill as he teaches and challenges you through the 6-week *Model Man* DVD Small Group Series. The study guide is full of challenging questions, discussions, self-study applications and action points! Follow Pastor Larry as he walks you through taking those steps necessary to go from integrity to legacy.

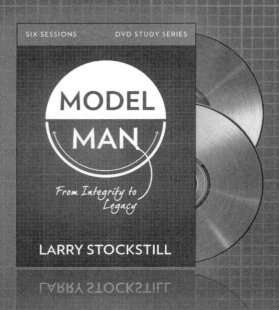

MODEL MAN: DVD STUDY SERIES
From Integrity to Legacy
by Larry Stockstill

In this 6-week DVD STUDY SERIES, Larry Stockstill will coach you in the journey from integrity to legacy with six 20-minute video sessions. Follow along each session using the *Model Man Study Guide* (sold separately). Get ready to be coached, challenged, broken, and rebuilt until God can see in you His greatest dream: the godly, long-term, influential, and powerful "model man"!

50 SMALL GROUP MEN'S LESSONS
by Larry Stockstill

These exciting and practical 50 lessons will walk you and your small group through 10 key lessons in each of the following topics: Leadership, Parables, Proverbs, Promises and Heroes. Each lesson is designed to discuss for 20 to 30 minutes and end with some challenging questions. Each man in your small group will learn what it takes to become a "model man."

LARRYSTOCKSTILL.COM

As a missionary in Africa for two years and a senior pastor for twenty eight years, Larry Stockstill's ministry has been global and local. His ministry now involves winning men to Christ (Model Man), planting local churches (Surge) and strengthening character in leaders (Remnant). With six children all in ministry, he and his wife Melanie minister together worldwide strengthening the marriages and families of today's Christian leaders.

What you can find at LarryStockstill.com:

1. Sermon Series
2. Individual Sermons
3. Books
4. Training Materials
5. Blogs
6. Newsletters
7. Book Pastor Larry for an event

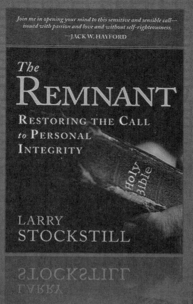

THE REMNANT
Restoring The Call To Personal Integrity
by Larry Stockstill

Throughout history, in every nation that has turned away from God, there has remained a remnant of righteous people: those who stayed true and did not forsake their covenant with Him. In his new book, Pastor Larry speaks to pastors and others in America who make up that remnant today. God is calling us to bring integrity back to ministry in America.

Pastor Larry Stockstill is restoring the call to personal integrity with his book *The Remnant*. The recent events of scandal in the church have shaken us to the core. Ministers, organizations, and Christians seem riddled with internal sin and secrets. Is there hope for change? Yes! God is raising up a remnant of believers to be a new example of irreproachable transparency and integrity in business, in ministry, and in marriage.

AVAILABLE FOR PURCHASE AT **BETHANYNETWORK.ORG**

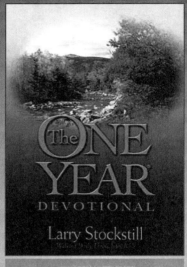

THE ONE YEAR DEVOTIONAL
Deepen Your Intimacy With God on a Daily Basis
by Larry Stockstill

"You can start building a deeper relationship with Christ today. Thi uplifting, easy-to-read devotional can be used each and every da to renew your faith and strengthen your understanding of God. The inspirational readings will guide you through the Bible in one year reminding you daily that you are never alone or without hope.

Start each day with *The One Year Devotional* and bring the comfort and joy of knowing God into your life all year long. Larry Stockstill invites you to embark on a journey with him this year through the exciting world o the Bible. Your life will never be the same!

THE SURGE
A Global Church-Planting Initiative
www.SurgeProject.com

"What is the greatest investment in missions in the world today?"

Larry Stockstill believes it is planting a national missionary to raise up a local church!

Come in to the world of Surge, a global church-planting movement touching all of the zones of the world. Surge is a bridge between Western supporters and national church planters worldwide and has planted over 20,000 village churches in the last ten years. Now its vision is to plant 30,000 new churches in the next ten years!

Your life, your small group, and your local church can be totally transformed by the simple process of planting a church anywhere in the world through the network of relationships forged through Surge.

Visit Surge's website www.surgeproject.com to find out more information on how to become a partner with Surge, or call our office 225.774.2000.

AVAILABLE FOR PURCHASE AT **BETHANYNETWORK.ORG**

BETHANY
COLLEGE

Where World Leaders Are Formed

ASSOCIATE OF ARTS IN CHRISTIAN LEADERSHIP

Local Church Experience

- Worship Leadership
- Live Production
- Hospitality and Event Planning

Pastoral Ministry

- Children's Ministry
- Youth Ministry
- Young Adult Ministry
- Pastoral Care and Outreach

Media and Creative Arts

- Graphic Design
- Web Design
- Video Production

BETHANY COLLEGE HAS OUTSTANDING ACADEMICS AND WILL EQUIP YOU FOR GOD'S CALLING ON YOUR LIFE. **WE WOULD LOVE TO** SEE YOU MATURE, DEVELOP, AND PLAY A PART IN WHAT GOD IS DOING ON OUR CAMPUS, IN OUR CHURCH, AND IN OUR CITY.

For more information call 225-412-5308 or visit
BETHANYCOLLEGE.NET

WE WOULD LIKE TO HEAR FROM YOU:

Has this book changed your situation or given you a new perspective?

Share your story with us, review@bethanypublishing.net

Have comments for the author?

Send them to author@bethanypublishing.net

Online Resources at

www.bethanypublishing.net

Sign Up For Our Newsletter at

www.bethanypublishing.net/newsletter
To Receive Coupons, Special Offers, & Most Recent News

Be Sure To Follow Us On:

Facebook: facebook.com/Bethanypublish
Twitter: @bethanypublish
Instagram: @bethanypublishing

NOTES